Visualization

Unlock Your Potential and Achieve Your Dreams

(An Easy & Proven Way to Reprogramming Your Subconscious Mind & Work)

Arthur Daniels

Published By **Cathy Nedrow**

Arthur Daniels

All Rights Reserved

Visualization: Unlock Your Potential and Achieve Your Dreams (An Easy & Proven Way to Reprogramming Your Subconscious Mind & Work)

ISBN 978-1-7752967-1-3

No part of this guidebook shall be reproduced in any form without permission in writing from the publisher except in the case of brief quotations embodied in critical articles or reviews.

Legal & Disclaimer

The information contained in this book is not designed to replace or take the place of any form of medicine or professional medical advice. The information in this book has been provided for educational & entertainment purposes only.

The information contained in this book has been compiled from sources deemed reliable, and it is accurate to the best of the Author's knowledge; however, the Author cannot guarantee its accuracy and validity and cannot be held liable for any errors or omissions. Changes are periodically made to this book. You must consult your doctor or get professional medical advice before using any of the suggested remedies, techniques, or information in this book.

Upon using the information contained in this book, you agree to hold harmless the Author from and against any damages, costs, and expenses, including any legal fees potentially resulting from the application of any of the information provided by this guide. This disclaimer applies to any damages or injury caused by the use and application, whether directly or indirectly, of any advice or information presented, whether for breach of contract, tort, negligence, personal injury, criminal intent, or under any other cause of action.

You agree to accept all risks of using the information presented inside this book. You need to consult a professional medical practitioner in order to ensure you are both able and healthy enough to participate in this program.

Table Of Contents

Chapter 1: Creative Visualization 1

Chapter 2: Faith as the Foundation 13

Chapter 3: The First Step to Realization .. 25

Chapter 4: God and the Power of Visualization 35

Chapter 5: Jesus' Light in the Art 45

Chapter 6: Discovering Your Inner Self ... 59

Chapter 7: Emotional Intelligence 64

Chapter 8: Understanding Visualization .. 79

Chapter 9: Creating the Ideal Visualization Environment 89

Chapter 10: Overcoming Obstacles in Visualization 105

Chapter 11: Visualization for Personal Growth 119

Chapter 12: Integrating Visualization into Your Daily Routine 128

Chapter 13: Visualization and Manifestation 139

Chapter 14: Associative Technique 147

Chapter 15: Wallet 167

Chapter 16: Soccer Ball 171

Chapter 1: Creative Visualization

1.1 Understanding Visualization.

In the great realm of human capability, few necessities personal the mysterious allure and transformative power that visualization holds. It serves as a bridge, one which connects the immaterial worlds of our thoughts and desires to the tangible effects in our out of doors global. But, like many gear that offer such profound change, the proper essence of visualization is regularly veiled in layers of misunderstandings and misconceptions.

To in reality draw close the idea of visualization, one ought to first undertaking past the surface-diploma information. At its middle, visualization isn't sincerely having a pipe dream or idle wishing. It is the deliberate exercising of forming unique, specific snap shots in the mind — snap shots that capture now not without a doubt factors of interest, but sounds, feelings, and even scents. It's the act of mentally embodying an final results or a choice, feeling its fact in the gift second, even earlier than its materialization within the physical realm.

Now, why would possibly this kind of seemingly simple intellectual exercising keep lots energy? Think of the mind as fertile soil. Every idea, each picture, is a seed planted interior this soil. When nurtured with notion and emotion, the ones seeds start to take root, influencing not just our internal country of being, but moreover drawing forth the conditions and circumstances in our outdoor global that resonate with those very images.

Misconceptions approximately visualization abound and they might create barriers for those searching for its blessings. One commonplace misconception is the idea that visualization is a form of escapism, a retreat from reality. This couldn't be further from the fact. Visualization, whilst practiced with motive and notion, is a proactive engagement with reality. It's now not approximately escaping the prevailing, but approximately shaping the destiny.

Another false impression revolves across the "strive" related to visualization. Many expect that the more strenuous and forceful their visualization, the extra powerful it is going to be. In fact, the power of visualization lies in its subtlety. It's about letting circulate and permitting the mind's eye to shade the popular truth, not forcing it. The emotion and perception that accompany this visualization are what lend it performance, no longer the sheer pressure of will.

Yet each different fallacy is the notion that visualization is quality a intellectual exercising, wreck loose motion. Some anticipate that thru using sincerely visualizing, without taking aligned motion, their desires will materialize. While visualization is immensely effective, it is handiest whilst used as a compass, guiding our moves and alternatives in the course of the belief of our predicted destiny.

It's moreover nicely worth noting that visualization isn't always restricted to the fulfillment of fabric or worldly goals. Its right capacity is determined out at the same time as it's far hired to shape one's man or woman, virtues, and internal kingdom of being. Imagine visualizing now not just a new domestic or manner, however a more affected person, compassionate, and statistics self. The outside changes that visualization can bring about are incredible, but the internal differences are truly profound.

Lastly, there is the misconception that visualization is a current-day fad, a modern-day discovery of self-assist authorities. In fact, visualization is an age-vintage exercise, embedded in the teachings of historic religious traditions and revered through manner of visionaries and leaders all through history. The terminologies might also have advanced, and the strategies subtle, but the center precept remains unchanged: the photographs we keep in our mind, on the equal time as suffused with perception and emotion, have the energy to form our fact.

In dispelling the ones misconceptions and deepening our knowledge, we smooth the route for a genuine engagement with the exercising of visualization. It's a journey that desires sincerity, perception, and staying power, but for individuals who embark upon it with an open coronary coronary coronary heart and thoughts, the rewards are beyond measure.

1.2. Historical Context.

As we step in addition into the depths of understanding visualization, it turns into easy that this isn't in reality a present day phenomenon or a cutting-edge approach. Its origins hint decrease lower back in the course of millennia, woven into the tapestries of historic civilizations and whispered via the teachings of non secular masters.

The ancients understood properly the energy of the mind. In the wonderful halls of Egypt,

Pharaohs and priests must mentally mission their dreams for abundance, safety, and divine connection, crafting tough seen stories at the partitions of their monuments. These have been not truely creative expressions but additionally symbolic reflections in their innermost visions. By visualizing and then externalizing their dreams, they believed they will impact the course of events, bringing their visions to life.

Further east, inside the verdant valleys of India, the yogis and sages harnessed the strength of Dharana, a Sanskrit term describing focused consciousness and visualization. Their ancient scriptures, the Vedas and Upanishads, make references to the profound impact of inner visions on outside reality. By diving deep into meditative states, the ones sages may want to visualize complicated patterns and emblems, guiding their religious journeys and influencing the electricity around them.

Similarly, within the misty mountains of ancient China, Daoist monks mentioned the usage of the 'Inner Eye' to appearance visions and goals, drawing upon the ones to stability the glide of Qi — the life pressure — in the direction of the body. Through their practices, they identified that with the beneficial resource of visualizing unique results or states of being, they might align their internal energies to take place the ones realities.

Even the terrific warriors of Sparta, appeared for their rigorous region and martial prowess, had been no strangers to the strength of visualization. Before battles, they might interact in rituals in which they mentally played out the upcoming battle, visualizing victory, and mentally making prepared themselves for the disturbing situations earlier.

We would be remiss not to well known the indigenous peoples of various lands, from the shamans of South America to the neighborhood tribes of North America.

Through their rituals and dances, they engaged in a collective form of visualization, invoking rain, an high-quality harvest, or the safety of their human beings. Their practices underscored the notion that the collective imagination of a community, whilst aligned with motive and emotion, can shape the very fabric of nature.

The Renaissance technology, a period recognized for its leaps in art and technological expertise, also noticed a revival in the appreciation of visualization. Visionaries like Leonardo da Vinci did not definitely draw what they found; they drew what they visualized. Their upgrades and works of artwork, which laid the inspiration for numerous modern-day marvels, have been birthed from the profound ability to visualise possibilities past the seemed horizons.

Though the contexts and practices severa within the direction of cultures and eras, the primary problem remember remained consistent: Visualization was a conduit to bridge the distance a few of the visible and the unseen, the regarded and the unknown. It modified into — and remains — a sacred dance a number of the inner international of desires, hopes, and aspirations, and the outdoor worldwide of genuine manifestation.

The awareness of those historic cultures serves as a poignant reminder. In cutting-edge-day international, wherein visualization techniques could probably appear as novelties or present day self-help gear, it's far vital to apprehend that we are simply rekindling an age-vintage flame — a flame that has illuminated human progress for a long term. By honoring and know-how the historic context of visualization, we gain a richer appreciation of its undying power and relevance in our adventure.

1.Three. The Science Behind Visualization.

As we journey from the annals of facts to the corridors of the thoughts, it will become vital to address the empirical underpinnings of visualization. While ancient civilizations and non secular instructors identified its efficiency thru intuition and experience, modern technological expertise gives a tangible framework, unveiling the exceptional procedures in which our thoughts responds to the act of visualization.

Peering into the complexities of the human mind famous a dynamic network of neurons, cells that speak via electric powered and chemical signals. One may also surprise, how does this form of system, positive by way of way of the usage of the laws of biology, lend itself to the airy approach of visualization? The key lies in a phenomenon referred to as neuroplasticity.

Neuroplasticity is the mind's wondrous ability to reorganize itself, forging new connections between neurons primarily based on our tales and thoughts. It defies the as quickly as-held belief that the character thoughts is static, unchanging. Instead, every idea, each vision, molds our neural panorama. In essence, whilst we visualize, we aren't definitely having a pipe dream; we're sculpting the very form of our mind.

A charming manifestation of this is visible in studies regarding athletes. Researchers determined that after athletes vividly visualize their usual performance, the identical neural pathways are activated as after they physically carry out the movement. This technique that a sprinter visualizing a race or a pianist imagining a trendy overall performance is mentally rehearsing, reinforcing neural pathways with none overt movement. The thoughts, it appears, struggles to differentiate among colourful creativeness and real enjoy.

But beyond mere intellectual rehearsal, the consequences of visualization ripple outwards, influencing our emotional and physiological states. The limbic tool, an ancient a part of our mind accountable for emotions, responds ardently to our visualizations. This is why imagining a annoying situation can bring about actual feelings of tension, whilst visualizing a peaceful scene can result in calmness. Herein lies a profound recognition: with the useful resource of manner of choosing our highbrow imagery, we wield the energy to dictate our emotional responses.

Furthermore, this emotional response catalyzes a cascade of hormonal modifications. Positive visualizations can growth ranges of serotonin and dopamine, neurotransmitters associated with happiness and well-being, at the same time as negative imagery can cause pressure hormones like cortisol. It's a tangible, biochemical testament to the adage: "As someone thinketh in his heart, so is he."

Chapter 2: Faith As The Foundation

2.1. The Nature of Faith.

Faith, a word often intertwined with religious doctrines and divine allegiances, reaches an extended way past the confines of sacred texts and locations of worship. In its purest form, faith transcends ritualistic beliefs, turning into the bedrock of our very life. To certainly recognize and harness the energy of visualization, we need to first respect the profound nature of faith, not as a theological accumulate, but as an innate human capability.

Imagine, if you will, a bridge spanning the chasm among our present day-day realities and our most cherished dreams. This bridge, invisible but invincible, is constructed of faith. Each plank, each nail, represents a notion in the unseen, a conviction in the however-to-be. While many also can pull away at the void below, the ones armed with religion tread fearlessly, assured of their excursion spot.

The universe, in all its complex beauty, operates on ideas. Just as gravity is unyielding, maintaining planets in orbit and anchoring us to the earth, faith too is a not unusual law. It is the stress that attracts the unseen into the arena of the seen. Wattles and Goddard, in their timeless teachings, alluded to this very principle. They stated the tangible strength of belief, of its capability to mold occasions and form destinies.

However, to harness religion, one must first understand its twin nature. On one hand, faith is a deep-seated notion in some thing unobservable, an unwavering believe within the eventual manifestation of our visions. But as an alternative, it is an active pressure, propelling us to take stimulated movement, to move in alignment with our beliefs.

Consider the farmer, who sows seeds within the area. He can't see the germination taking location beneath the soil, but he waters the sphere diligently, trusting inside the eventual bloom. This is faith — the marriage of notion and motion. He does not preference; he is aware of. And this understanding, with out doubt and hesitation, is the crux of proper faith.

Such faith isn't always a reserve of the non secular or spiritual elite. Each one folks possesses this strong stress. When a toddler takes its first step, it's far an act of faith. When an entrepreneur invests in a vision, it's an act of religion. Every second, every breath, is steeped in faith. The coronary coronary heart beats, the lungs expand, now not out of preference, but out of a deep-seated notion in the subsequent moment, the subsequent breath.

Yet, it's miles crucial to distinguish amongst blind religion and the empowering faith we communicate right here. Blind religion clings to beliefs without statistics, without questioning. It's rigid, frequently leading to stagnation. Empowering religion, however, is dynamic. It's a conscious choice, born out of information and enjoy. It's malleable, growing and evolving with each venture, every triumph.

So, how does one domesticate such faith? It starts offevolved with know-how our innate worthiness, recognizing that we are not mere spectators inside the theatre of lifestyles, but co-creators. Each notion, each vision, sends ripples for the duration of the cloth of lifestyles. By acknowledging this strength and aligning our moves with our ideals, we nurture our religion.

Moreover, religion thrives in an environment of exceptional reinforcement. Surrounding oneself with memories of triumph, with people who've traversed the path of notion, strengthens our solve. Every story of fulfillment, every tale of manifestation, serves as a testomony to the strength of religion.

As we journey ahead, allow us to hold religion as our compass, guiding us through the mists of doubt and uncertainty. Let or not it is the torch that illuminates our route, revealing the steps to our dreams. For in knowledge and harnessing the character of faith, we release the doorways to endless opportunities, placing the level for the chapters that lie ahead.

In the unfolding tapestry of this exploration, religion emerges no longer definitely as a bankruptcy however because the very thread that weaves collectively desires and fact. With this foundation, we're poised to delve deeper into the intricacies of visualization, fortified through the unyielding power of belief.

2.2. The Link among Faith and Visualization.

The dance amongst faith and visualization is one of profound splendor, a harmonious ballet wherein each enhances the possibility. Faith, as we've got come to recognize, is the bedrock, the unyielding basis upon which our dreams discover footing. Visualization, however, gives the colourful imagery, the vibrant tapestry upon which our aspirations take shape and colour.

Consider, for a 2d, the hold close artist. Before a unmarried brush stroke graces the canvas, there exists within the mind's eye a sparkly imaginative and prescient of the final masterpiece. Yet, it is not merely the imaginative and prescient that brings the painting to existence. It's the unwavering notion, the unshakable faith, that every stroke, every hue, will take location the imaginative and prescient as conceived. Without this faith, the artist may additionally additionally falter, the brush may additionally waver, and the painting may remain an unfulfilled dream.

In the nation-states of our minds, we are all artists, portray our futures with the comb of visualization. Yet, it is religion that infuses this vision with life. Visualization provides the blueprint, the right map of our goals, while faith energizes this map, turning precis mind into tangible critiques.

Visualization with out faith is comparable to a seed with out soil. It possesses functionality, fine, but lacks the nurturing environment to germinate and flourish. Faith, in its nurturing encompass, affords the fertile ground for our visualized wants to take root and develop. It assures the coronary heart and mind that what is visible within the silent chambers of our creativeness can and will materialize in the colourful place of life.

Yet, how does this alchemy work? How does religion expand the energy of visualization? The answer lies within the very nature of notion. When we possess unwavering faith, our unconscious thoughts accepts the visualized dream as an imminent reality. This reputation sends forth ripples, vibrations that align with the frequencies of our dreams. In essence, religion transforms highbrow snap shots into lively blueprints, equipped to materialize inside the physical worldwide.

There is a connection among religion and visualization and a deep dating. It is important to feel the choice fulfilled, to immerse your self within the feelings of the desired cease result. What is this if now not faith in movement? It's one thing to look a dream; it's miles each distinctive completely to feel it, to stay it inside the gift 2d.

Moreover, the amplifying effect of religion on visualization can be likened to sunlight hours on a magnifying glass. A magnifying glass by myself can consciousness, can provide clarity. But at the equal time as daytime - representing religion - passes through it, the focused mild turns into amazing sufficient to ignite hearth. Similarly, our visualizations, even as infused with the acute light of faith, grow to be terrific forces of manifestation.

Visualization trains the thoughts, guiding it closer to readability of purpose and intensity of choice. Faith, then, assures the coronary coronary heart that the path visualized isn't best feasible but inevitable. This harmonious combination of coronary coronary heart and mind, of emotion and imagery, gadgets the diploma for remarkable manifestations.

One can also ask: If visualization is the seed and faith the soil, what then is the water and daylight that nurture the growth? The answer: Emotion and movement. But it's miles religion that ensures that the emotion is wonderful, the movement inspired. Faith whispers in our ear that each attempt, every thought in step with our visualized aim, brings us a step towards its cognizance.

While visualization sketches the dream, religion breathes existence into it. Together, they shape an unbeatable duo, a partnership that ensures now not sincerely the visualization of dreams however their inevitable recognition. As we journey ahead on this exploration, let us keep in mind to preserve each near, expertise that during their union lies the crucial thing to unlocking our actual capability.

2.Three. Cultivating Stronger Faith

Faith, that ethereal but essential pressure, isn't truly a present bestowed upon the selected few. Instead, it's far a muscle, ready to be flexed and bolstered. Much just like the artist refining their craft or the musician schooling their scales, so too are we able to domesticate and pork up our notion. The route to a more profound faith is paved with workout, introspection, and devoted motion.

In our adventure thru the landscape of visualization and its strong manifestations, the importance of an unwavering faith becomes ever clearer. For the dreamer who gazes into the future with preference however reveals the shadow of doubt creeping in, there are practices to banish those uncertainties and supply a lift to 1's perception. Let us delve into those practices, expertise that with each step, we weave a more potent tapestry of faith.

1. Immersion in Positive Environments: Surrounding oneself with positivity and like-minded human beings is paramount. When we immerse ourselves in environments that echo our aspirations and beliefs, our religion is not superb reinforced however additionally

contemplated all over again to us. Such environments become crucibles wherein our beliefs are tested, purified, and then solidified.

2. Affirmations and Autosuggestions: Words wield power. The terms we repeat to ourselves, both aloud or in the silent chambers of our minds, mildew our belief structures. By crafting affirmations that resonate with our goals and repeating them with conviction, we embed these ideals deeper inner our unconscious. Over time, the ones repeated affirmations emerge as our fact, riding away doubt and organising religion.

three. Meditative Reflection: In the stillness of meditation, feasible tap into the large reservoirs of internal information. By regularly putting apart moments for mirrored photo, we permit ourselves to connect with our innermost dreams and beliefs. This practice not simplest silences outdoor noise but moreover amplifies the voice of our inner conviction, nurturing the seeds of faith.

four. Celebrate Small Victories: Often, in our quest for large achievements, we overlook the smaller victories that pepper our journey. Recognizing and celebrating those moments fortifies our belief inside the huge imaginative and prescient. Each achievement, irrespective of how minor, serves as proof of our capabilities, pushing us to dream large and agree with stronger.

5. Continuous Learning and Growth: When we equip ourselves with know-how and know-how, we create a foundation on which our faith can stand. Seeking understanding, exploring severa philosophies, and knowledge the complex dance a few of the conscious and unconscious mind permit us to look the larger image. This broader attitude diminishes doubts and paves the manner for a extra profound faith.

Chapter 3: The First Step To Realization

3.1. Defining Awareness.

In the massive expanse of the human psyche, wherein desires weave into realities and aspirations beckon from the horizon, there exists a delicate filament of mild, illuminating the proper right here and now. This luminous thread, regularly neglected in our race inside the path of destiny goals, is recognition. While visualization serves as our compass to far flung beaches, it is awareness that anchors us, reminding us of the sacredness of the triumphing second, the very canvas upon which destiny visions take form.

Awareness, in its purest essence, transcends mere alertness or knowledge. It is not pretty much spotting one's environment or being attuned to the sensory opinions. Instead, it touches a deeper realm, a silent area wherein one is simply gift, experiencing life no longer as a passive spectator however as an lively participant. It's a country of being where each heartbeat, every breath, each concept resonates with the coronary heart beat of the universe.

The international spherical us brims with distractions. Sounds, points of hobby, emotions, and mind continuously clamor for our hobby, regularly pulling us away from the instant. Yet, amidst this cacophony, reputation stands as a serene sentinel, gently guiding our cognizance again to the now. It reminds us that at the equal time because the beyond is a memory and the destiny a thriller, the prevailing is a gift, one that holds the keys to our private alterations.

Imagine, for a fast 2nd, an artist status in advance than a smooth canvas. The artist, complete of visions of what the canvas ought to become, is tempted to dive at once into creation. But, if he pauses, if he's taking a 2nd to truly revel in the canvas, to be aware of its texture, its nuances, its very being, then every brushstroke that follows will become a dance of harmony, a symphony of advent. Such is the strength of focus. It enriches our moves, making them now not really method to an give up, however sacred rituals in themselves.

For the individual embarking on the journey of visualization, records the place of interest is paramount. Visualization isn't pretty lots crafting destiny realities, however approximately deeply feeling and facts the present, for it's far in the intensity of the present 2d that the seeds of the destiny are sown. The clearer our awareness of the present, the greater awesome our visualizations come to be, resonating with the truest dreams of our hearts.

Yet, one ought to possibly question, how does one cultivate such heightened popularity, particularly in a international that continually vies for our hobby? The pathway to interest is as hard because it is simple. It begins offevolved with silence. Not in reality the absence of sound, but the stilling of the inner chatter, the quietening of the relentless mind. Moments of stillness, in which one certainly is, with out judgments, unfastened from the binds of the beyond or the attraction of the destiny, function gateways to heightened attention.

Breathing, a consistent rhythm of existence, gives some different portal. By honestly specializing in one's breath, feeling its ebb and glide, its moderate upward push and fall, you may be able to anchor oneself inside the gift. It serves as a reminder that lifestyles, in its essence, is a chain of moments, and to virtually live is to be completely determined in each of them.

In our quest for undertaking our desires, it's far smooth to wander off in the appeal of the destiny, to be continuously propelled ahead with the aid of our goals. However, as we delve deeper into the artwork of visualization and the gadget at our disposal, it's miles essential to go through in mind that every dream, every vision, is rooted in the now. The gift 2nd, with its endless opportunities, is the crucible in which our future takes shape.

As we keep on this journey, weaving collectively the threads of visualization, religion, and notion, permit us to not neglect the silent power of attention. For in actually know-how the winning, in being absolutely alive in the now, we no longer best increase our journey however furthermore deliver our future visions into sharper popularity, making them tangible realities in the tapestry of our lives.

3.2. Benefits of Enhanced Awareness.

Within the giant corridors of human recognition, wherein mind flutter like leaves on a wind-swept day, there can be a profound depth that remains in large part unexplored. This place, teeming with unbridled capacity, is illuminated with the resource of the mild moderate of interest. As previously explored, defining and know-how this hobby is foundational. Now, permit us to delve into the bountiful blessings it bestows upon its cultivators.

An enhanced experience of interest, much like a finely tuned device, transforms every aspect of existence. Consider the profound impact of actually listening. In a global wherein conversations often become mere exchanges of terms, to pay attention with heightened focus approach to apprehend the unsaid, to experience the emotions carried with the aid of the breeze of terms, and to actually connect to the soul of every specific. This exceptional of listening, born from natural interest, fosters deeper relationships, permitting bonds to be woven from threads of actual know-how and empathy.

Moreover, the world of creativity is drastically enriched via this heightened attention. Artists, writers, and creators from diverse fields have often spoken of moments on the same time as suggestion flows results. These are moments at the same time as they may be deeply rooted inside the present, completely attuned to their internal international, and receptive to the universe's whispers. Enhanced interest acts as a bridge, connecting the conscious mind to the reservoirs of creativity lying dormant within the unconscious. It permits the writer to tap into visions, ideas, and emotions that would in any other case stay obscured via the clutter of normal thoughts.

Shifting our gaze to the field of desire-making, it will become glaring that selections crafted from an area of profound focus have a tendency to resonate with one's actual self. Such options are not actually reactions to outdoor stimuli, nor are they brought about unduly via manner of fleeting feelings. Instead, they emerge from a serene space of clarity, wherein the character can understand the broader tapestry of lifestyles and apprehend the implications of every preference.

And, of route, most essential to our discourse is the harmonious dating amongst better recognition and powerful visualization. A clean, nevertheless mind, unperturbed by way of using manner of distractions, turns into a fertile ground for planting the seeds of visualization. The visions conceived inside the type of nation of recognition are colourful, precise, and charged with motive. They are not mere daydreams or fleeting whims; they carry about the weight of right preference and the clarity of motive. By cultivating recognition, one have to preserve those visions steadfastly, nurturing them with hobby and perception till they blossom into tangible realities.

The exercising of mindfulness, a shape of meditation rooted in heightened recognition of the triumphing, in addition underscores the transformative electricity of this country of attention. Mindfulness, often lauded for its recuperation consequences on the thoughts and body, serves as a testament to the profound advantages of living within the now. Reduced stress, greater appropriate emotional law, extended cognitive flexibility – those are but most of the various boons that rise up from frequently immersing oneself within the ocean of the existing.

Furthermore, a deep sense of contentment and inner peace accompanies more potent attention. By in reality experiencing each 2d, one realizes the temporary nature of life's usaand downs. Challenges are perceived now not as insurmountable limitations however as levels that, too, shall skip. Similarly, joys are savored with a deeper appreciation, understanding that they may be ephemeral gadgets to be loved. This balanced attitude, born from profound reputation, paves the manner for a life lived with grace, resilience, and gratitude.

Lastly, recall the ripple effect such recognition can create within the broader spectrum of society. Individuals who feature from a vicinity of deep hobby usually will be predisposed to exude positivity, empathy, and knowledge. Their interactions, alternatives, and actions, advocated with the aid of the use of this holistic attitude, can inspire others to are seeking comparable depths inner themselves, putting in movement a chain of transformation.

In the labyrinth of lifestyles, wherein infinite paths beckon and myriad distractions abound, the slight of popularity acts as a guiding celebrity. It invites people to adventure inward, to find out realms of awareness hitherto uncharted, and to harness the boundless benefits that lie therein. The adventure, in spite of the truth that intensely personal, has the capacity to reshape now not simply person destinies, however the very material of society. The key lies in spotting, cultivating, and cherishing this profound awareness. For internal its depths, the secrets and techniques to a lifestyles of motive, satisfaction, and success appearance beforehand to.

Chapter 4: God And The Power Of Visualization

4.1. Visualization and Divinity.

In the huge expanse of human records, a golden thread has continuously woven its manner thru the tapestry of our lifestyles, shimmering with the promise of unseen geographical regions and non secular awakenings. This thread, although every so often obscured by using the ebbs and flows of societal progression, generally re-emerges, as radiant as ever. This thread is our intrinsic choice to connect to the Divine, to understand our area inside the grand cosmic dance, and to harness the immeasurable strength that the universe bestows upon us. At the intersection of this divine connection and our aware intentions lies the robust exercising of visualization.

Often, at the same time as one embarks upon the route of visualization, the number one recognition revolves across the tangible, the worldly, and the right away perceivable. Yet, past the horizon of cloth dreams and concrete aspirations, there exists a realm wherein visualization takes on a hue of sacredness, turning into a bridge among the finite and the limitless.

Consider the profound mystics and sages of historical civilizations. Delving deep into meditative trances, they painted shiny pictures in their minds, not of worldly riches or temporal successes, however of divine encounters, cosmic revelations, and non secular enlightenment. Their visualizations were now not mere tools for manifesting dreams but sacred rites, drawing them inside the path of the heartbeat of the universe.

The motive visualization holds such religious performance stems from its very nature. At its center, visualization is the act of introduction in the thoughts's sanctum. It mirrors, in a microcosmic enjoy, the very act of Divine Creation. Just because of the reality the universe modified into birthed from a imaginative and prescient, a divine perception, so too are our realities fashioned with the useful resource of the visions we nurture internal.

Every act of visualization, then, turns into a homage to this divine process of introduction. When one closes their eyes and visualizes, they tap into this often taking vicinity cutting-edge pressure, aligning their power with the cosmos. This alignment no longer best amplifies the energy of 1's visualizations but moreover deepens their religious connection, turning each act of visualization proper right into a sacred ritual.

There's a silent, almost reverent beauty in the manner. Envisioning a preferred reality, one would possibly not without a doubt venture desires onto the universe's canvas. Instead, they co-create with the Divine, merging their intentions with the boundless energy of introduction. It's a dance of the soul with the cosmos, in which every step, each twirl, is guided via manner of the song of divine goal.

To method visualization as a non secular workout is to elevate it past mere approach. It turns into an act of faith, a testomony to the notion that the universe listens, responds, and co-creates. Just as a sculptor lovingly molds clay, giving shape to what became formless, the visualizer molds their fact, shaping it with the palms of motive and the spirit of religion.

Embracing the religious size of visualization moreover infuses the workout with a sense of motive and sanctity. No longer are visualizations fleeting daydreams or mere wishful questioning. They turn out to be prayers, offerings to the universe, bearing the soul's personal yearnings. Each visualization, as a end result, is an act of take delivery of as actual with, a give up to the cosmic waft, an confirmation of one's divine nature.

Yet, it's miles vital to technique this union of visualization and divinity with humility. For at the equal time as one wields the energy to shape truth, they live forever a part of the grand cosmic format, a unmarried study in the symphony of life. This records instills within the visualizer a deep reverence for the technique, ensuring they never lose sight of the divine tapestry to which they make a contribution.

The adventure of visualization, at the same time as visible via the lens of spirituality, will become infinitely richer. It's now not pretty lots manifesting dreams however also approximately deepening one's connection to the Divine, knowledge the rhythms of the universe, and aligning with its grand layout. Each second spent in visualization becomes a sacred communion, a melding of the soul with the cosmos, a dance of electricity and aim.

In this sacred area, the bounds a number of the self and the universe blur. The visualizer realizes that they're no longer only a passive observer however an active player within the divine play of creation. And with this recognition comes a profound feel of empowerment, a recognition of 1's divine nature, and the infinite opportunities that lie inside.

Thus, as we tread the direction of visualization, let us take into account its sacred roots, its non secular essence. Let every visualization be a testament to our faith, a mirrored image of our divinity, and a step inside the course of the cosmic dance that binds us all. For inside the realm of the spirit, visualization will become now not best a device however a sacred ceremony, a bridge to the Divine, and a testomony to the boundless electricity of introduction that lies indoors us all.

4.2. Prayer vs. Visualization.

In the complex tapestry of human non secular practices, threads emerge, every luminous in their essence, but super of their weaving. These are the practices of prayer and visualization. To the untrained eye, they may seem as one, every beckoning the limitless, each searching out alignment with the cosmos. But a higher examination famous a profound dance of cause, approach, and very last outcomes. Herein lies the beauty and energy of expertise those practices: no longer as fighters, however as harmonious gadgets in the orchestra of non secular connection.

Prayer, in its many office work and traditions, is a venerable exercise that frequently seeks communion with the Divine. It is an act of humility, a engaging in out, an acknowledgment of a stress extra than oneself. When one prays, they stand at the threshold of their non-public being, casting their hopes, fears, gratitude, and pleas into the tremendous expanse of the universe. There's an innate give up in prayer, an know-how that whilst we very very own free will, there are factors past our manipulate, geographical regions wherein best faith can tread. The supplicant, through their phrases or silent utterances, seeks steerage, intervention, or genuinely a deeper reference to the divine essence.

Visualization, as an opportunity, is an act of conscious creation. It's the paintings of painting the canvas of reality with the brushstrokes of the mind's private desires and intentions. Where prayer regularly seeks to apprehend or receive the divine will, visualization seeks to mildew and shape one's fact in alignment with private or typical intentions. It isn't a passive act but considered one in all active advent. It taps into the big reservoir of our innate powers, urging us to form our destinies, to align our energies with the universe, and to show up our internal maximum desires.

Yet, in spite of these variations, there exists a confluence, a meeting aspect in which prayer and visualization converge. Both practices perform at the precept that perception, purpose, and emotion can effect truth. Both consider inside the interconnectedness of all subjects, within the concept that the man or woman soul and the cosmos are frequently entwined.

In this union of practices, one may want to possibly even argue that visualization is an evolution of prayer. It's prayer in motion. While conventional prayer places the outcome in the palms of the Divine, trusting in a better plan, visualization empowers the person to be an lively player inside the unfolding of their destiny. Yet, this doesn't make one superior to the opportunity. Instead, they offer outstanding paths to the identical holiday spot: a harmonious life in song with the universe.

Another shared trait is the deep emotional resonance every practices elicit. Whether it's miles the profound peace one feels while surrendering to a better strength in prayer or the burning preference that fuels visualization, emotion is the crucible. It's the catalyst that propels the ones practices into the location of the tangible, making summary desires palpable and weaving intentions into the cloth of fact.

Consider the device of every. When one prays, they frequently visualize their hopes coming to fruition, they see the recuperation of a loved one, the choice of a undertaking, or the attainment of a purpose. Simultaneously, in visualization, there may be often an unspoken prayer, a choice that the universe will conspire, that energies will align, and that what is imagined might be manifested.

Yet, it's miles crucial to navigate those practices with a balanced attitude. While visualization places emphasis on our capability and our feature as co-creators, it's also a reminder of our divine essence. And in spite of the fact that prayer might be seen as surrender, it's also a testomony to the human spirit's resilience and its everlasting connection to the infinite.

Chapter 5: Jesus' Light In The Art

5.1. The Teachings of Jesus.

In the resplendent realm of spiritual concept, the instructions of Jesus stand luminous, casting a transcendent moderate upon the human soul's pathways. They aren't clearly tenets of faith but profound thoughts, guiding people within the course of a life infused with cause, love, and abundance. Yet, internal those teachings lies an often-unnoticed measurement, one that serves as a bedrock for the powerful exercise of visualization.

When Jesus said, "The nation of heaven is internal you," He illuminated a truth, resounding through a while, that the outside international mirrors the internal realm. The "u . S .", He located is not a miles off realm but an inner sanctum of attention, good sized with possibilities prepared to be determined out. It is in this sacred place that the seeds of visualization discover fertile ground.

Delving deeper into His words, "Ask, and it will likely be given you; attempting to find, and ye shall discover; knock, and it'll be opened unto you," well-known an affirmation of lifestyles's benevolent nature. Here, Jesus encapsulates the essence of visualization. To "ask" is to define one's goals with readability, to are looking for is to align moves with the ones desires, and to knock indicates the unwavering perception in the approaching manifestation of one's visions.

Moreover, on the same time as Jesus walked upon the waters, have become water into wine, or healed the unwell, He have become now not just acting miracles for the spectacle. Each act, imbued with deeper symbolic meanings, showcased the infinite opportunities at the identical time as human religion aligns with divine purpose. These were not without a doubt acts of divine intervention; they had been powerful visualizations manifested in bodily truth.

Consider the Sermon on the Mount, wherein He expounds, "Blessed are individuals who hunger and thirst for righteousness, for they may be filled." This isn't just a call for ethical integrity however an acknowledgment that people who yearn, who vividly visualize a existence of righteousness, shall see their aspirations come to existence. Their internal visions, fueled via purity of motive, materialize in the canvas of the outdoor worldwide.

In each specific profound education, Jesus states, "Therefore I can help you recognise, some thing you ask for in prayer, remember that you have acquired it, and it'll be yours." Herein lies the very essence of visualization. The act of believing that one has already acquired their coronary heart's preference, even in advance than its physical manifestation, paves the manner for its attention. This is not mere wishful questioning but a robust alignment of one's internal vibrational frequency with that of the favored final consequences.

To in fact understand the interplay among Jesus's teachings and visualization, one should draw close the concept of faith, which He so often emphasized. Faith, in this context, isn't always a passive perception however an lively take delivery of as authentic with, a aware choice to look beyond the apparent and understand the countless potentials that lie in wait. Through religion, one acknowledges the unseen, giving substance to their visions, making the intangible tangible.

The parable of the mustard seed further amplifies this idea. The mustard seed, even though minuscule, grows proper into a sprawling tree. Similarly, a imaginative and prescient, irrespective of how small or inconspicuous, while nurtured with faith, can burgeon into a incredible reality. It's a testament to the electricity of perception, a gentle reminder that in the realm of advent, duration or price is of little end result; it is the depth of belief and readability of imaginative and prescient that maintain sway.

Delve deeper, and one discerns that Jesus's existence, in its entirety, changed into a masterclass in visualization. His adventure, from His humble transport in a manger to His crucifixion and subsequent resurrection, shows the cyclical nature of desires. They are birthed in simplicity, often face challenges and crucibles, quality to rise all yet again, more potent, and profound.

Drawing parallels a number of the instructions of Jesus and the art work of visualization is not an exercise in spiritual recontextualization. Instead, it's miles a reputation that spiritual truths, no matter the generation they had been propounded in, hold kernels of information applicable to modern practices.

In embracing Jesus's teachings, people do not merely turn out to be recipients of non secular information; they turn out to be co-creators, energetic humans within the grand dance of creation. Through visualization, aligned with the ideas He championed, they mold their reality, not as mere mortals however as divine beings, harnessing the limitless potentials of the universe.

In the terms and deeds of Jesus, one discerns a roadmap, no longer only for religious salvation however for a life enough with dreams discovered out and visions manifested. Through His teachings, visualization emerges not as a brand new-age approach but as an age-vintage workout, deeply entrenched in the non secular facts of humankind.

five.2 Parables and Visualization.

In the wealthy tapestry of biblical teachings, parables shine as beacons, illuminating profound truths through smooth, but poignant memories. These stories, gracefully woven with layers of popularity, beckon the discerning heart and mind to delve deeper, seeking out no longer without a doubt the overt narrative but the covert requirements they enshrine. Among the ones thoughts lies a treasure often left out—the paintings and essence of visualization.

Take, as an example, the myth of the sower. As seeds fell on numerous grounds—a few on the wayside, a few on stony locations, others among thorns, and however others on unique floor—their fates diverse. Here, the seed represents the nascent visions and dreams one harbors. The ground symbolizes america of the us of 1's mind and coronary coronary heart. Without fertile floor, even the maximum effective seed (or vision) withers away. The nourishment of religion, perseverance, and favorable situations lets in it to flourish. It teaches that the soil of our hobby need to be tended to, ensuring it's far receptive to the visions we desire to cultivate.

Or maintain in thoughts the parable of the abilties. Entrusted with varying portions, servants make one of a kind options. The one which buried his abilities in the floor symbolizes folks who, out of worry or complacency, suppress their goals and visions. In assessment, those who extended their talents resonate with folks that actively nurture, refine, and growth their visions, thereby actualizing them within the global's theatre. This parable is a clarion call to movement, urging one to no longer genuinely harbor visions however to behave upon them, to put money into them, expertise that the universe rewards the ambitious and the diligent.

The parable of the prodigal son, too, holds gemstones of visualization. The extra youthful son, after squandering his wealth, envisions a pass returned to his father's residence, no longer as a son, however as a humble servant. Yet, in his heart, he held a glimmer of need, a imaginative and prescient of forgiveness and popularity. It's this vision that propels him ahead. When he ultimately returns, his father's encompass surpasses his maximum effective visualizations. This story accentuates the energy of redemption and the idea that no matter how bleak one's gift may additionally appear, preserving onto a clean, satisfactory vision can result in consequences past one's wildest desires.

The parable of the mustard seed, referred to in advance, is well simply worth revisiting. A minuscule seed, at the same time as sown, burgeons right into a sprawling tree, imparting safe haven to birds. This is the quintessence of visualization. From a tiny, nearly insignificant vision, with the proper nurturing, can emerge a truth sizable and influential. Size, initial assets, or modern-day times depend little. It's the unwavering faith, the relentless nurturing, and the readability of the imaginative and prescient that decide the rate of its popularity.

The parable of the hidden treasure, in which a person discovers a treasure in a region and sells all he owns to shop for that vicinity, highlights the power of a compelling vision. Here, the treasure represents one's desires, and the arena symbolizes the journey or the approach. Once one recognizes the rate in their vision (the treasure), they will be inclined to make sacrifices, to invest their all, know-how that the rewards—each intangible and tangible—are amazing.

Delving into the ones parables, a pattern emerges. The biblical testimonies are not clearly tales; they may be metaphors, allegories that, while deciphered, offer profound insights into the individual of dreams, visions, and their manifestations. They underscore the importance of readability, religion, motion, nurturing, or perhaps the willingness to make sacrifices in the quest to convert visions into realities.

Moreover, the ones parables characteristic undying reminders that visualization isn't a present day-day-day construct, a fleeting style of modern self-assist geographical regions. It's a workout, an paintings, deeply rooted in religious traditions, echoed via a while in myriad methods, watching for the discerning seeker to understand and harness its strength.

Drawing belief from the ones parables, one realizes that the adventure of visualization is each sacred and transformative. Like the characters in these reminiscences, every character holds the ability to chart a journey from mere dreaming to tangible interest. All it calls for is a coronary coronary heart whole of religion, a mind replete with readability, and the spirit's resilience.

In essence, the Bible, via its parables, offers no longer definitely spiritual know-how however a roadmap to manifesting one's goals, making it obvious that the divine dreams for each soul to understand its visions, to stay a existence now not of mediocrity however of class.

five.Three. Walking with Jesus

In the quiet chambers of 1's soul, there may be a mild that beckons. This radiant stress, acquainted to many, emanates from the training and life of Jesus Christ. To walk with Jesus isn't always simply a religious pursuit however a profound religious adventure, allowing one's innermost goals and aspirations to align with the divine purpose.

Jesus, within the direction of His existence, manifested the essence of a visionary. The miracles He completed, the truths He shared, were not merchandise of mere physicality however stemmed from a profound know-how of non secular regulation. He visualized a international healed, redeemed, and brought again into harmony with the Father. By anchoring His ideals inside the non secular realm, the fabric worldwide in truth observed healthy.

One may possibly contemplate, "How can I too harness this divine data in my visualization workout?" It is by means of using traveling side via aspect with Jesus, letting His teachings remove darkness from the direction. When one aligns their visions with the instructions of love, compassion, and religion that Jesus embodied, they faucet into a pressure a ways extra than any human purpose. They touch the countless.

Jesus as fast as stated, "Truly I will let you understand, if you have religion as small as a mustard seed, you may say to this mountain, 'Move from proper here to there,' and it will flow into. Nothing may be not possible for you." This wasn't most effective a lesson in faith but a revelation of the energy of visualization. Here, He changed into guiding us to look beyond the prevailing, to study a reality converted by means of manner of religion, and to arise that imaginative and prescient with unwavering notion.

When embarking on the journey of visualization, one ought to keep in mind Jesus beside them, guiding their each step. Visualize Him on foot at the seashores of Galilee, talking phrases of attention, recovery the sick, and raising the useless. In those visualizations, discover now not truly the miracles, but the underlying spiritual truths. The water He walked upon symbolizes the turbulent feelings and doubts that many face. By strolling upon them, Jesus shows that with religion, we can also upward thrust above our challenges.

While the world also can gift its set of trials and tribulations, the strength to convert those conditions lies within. When confronted with an obstacle, in area of viewing it as a trouble, see it as Jesus did: an possibility for boom, a call to elevate one's faith, and a task to visualize a better final results. Let His teachings be the lamp unto your toes, guiding your visualizations towards the manifestation of your truest goals.

Furthermore, consist of the silences and the moments of stillness. In those quiet moments, Jesus regularly retreated to commune with the Father. It became in this sacred communion that He drew His strength and readability. Similarly, as one seeks to appear their visions, it is essential to discover moments of solitude, to hook up with the divine, and to listen. For inside the silent whispers of the soul, the truest visions are birthed.

Chapter 6: Discovering Your Inner Self
6.1. The Inner Realm

Deep internal anybody lies a realm, fantastic and complicated, wherein desires take shape, mind ebb and go together with the drift, and feelings paint colourful landscapes. This is the inner realm, an introspective universe wherein the very essence of one's being is living. It is a global untouched with the useful resource of way of outdoor times, a sanctuary in which the soul whispers its internal maximum desires and the spirit dances freely. To without a doubt recognise the power of visualization and faith, it's far paramount to first apprehend this inner universe, for it's far the birthplace of all manifestations.

Imagine, for a 2d, a canvas — smooth and unmarred. Every person possesses this type of canvas inside, wherein the brushstrokes of their ideals, desires, fears, and hopes craft complicated paintings. This canvas isn't static. It changes, evolves, and transforms with each notion entertained, each emotion felt, and each experience encountered. Every soul's canvas is unique, wearing imprints of past opinions, current-day-day aspirations, and future desires.

One may probable marvel, why is that this inner realm so vital? The solution is straightforward but profound: the out of doors international is however a reflected photo of the inner. The situations one unearths in their surroundings, the conditions they navigate, or perhaps the people they lure are all mirrors, reflecting the vibrancy or the chaos of their internal international. Therefore, to persuade the out of doors, one must first grasp the internal.

Now, delving into this realm isn't a mere act of introspection. It is a sacred adventure, a pilgrimage to the middle of one's being. It calls for courage, for internal its depths lie no longer certainly the desires and joys, however moreover the shadows and fears. Yet, confronting the ones shadows, embracing everything of this realm, is the important issue to right transformation.

The beauty of the inner realm is its malleability. While it holds recollections of the beyond and projections of the destiny, it is not bound with the useful useful resource of them. With aware motive, viable reshape this realm, mould it to align with their maximum aspirations. But how? The tools are those already mentioned: unwavering faith and robust visualization. By keeping a easy imaginative and prescient, fueled through way of herbal religion, the inner canvas starts to shift, converting its sunglasses and styles to resonate with that imaginative and prescient.

Many high-quality sages have spoken of the importance of inner concord. For on the same time as there may be harmony internal, it manifests without. This harmony is performed while the ideals held, the thoughts entertained, and the emotions felt are in alignment with one's genuine dreams. It's a symphony in which each word, each chord, resonates with the song of the soul.

However, one want to take into account that the journey to analyzing the internal realm is ongoing. It's a dance, on occasion smooth, from time to time stumbling, between the conscious and the subconscious, the appeared and the unknown. And even as the adventure is deeply non-public, its rewards are everyday. A mastered inner realm radiates its mild outward, influencing now not just the character's lifestyles but additionally touching the lives of those round them.

In this age, in which outside distractions are hundreds, turning inward might also additionally seem counterintuitive. The cacophony of the outer worldwide frequently drowns the whispers of the inner. But therein lies the mission and the reward. For folks that dare to adventure indoors, to discover the vastness in their inner realm, find out no longer really themselves however additionally the keys to manifesting their grandest goals.

It is said that each first-rate journey begins offevolved with a unmarried step. In the quest to harness the energy of the universe, to seem desires into fact, that step is inward. To define one's internal international is not definitely to understand it however to take the reins, to emerge as the artist of one's canvas, to be the composer of one's symphony.

For inside the coronary coronary heart of the internal realm lies no longer just the essence of the person, but the essence of creation itself. And understanding this realm, mastering its intricacies, is the course to no longer just personal transformation but to shaping the very material of truth. Thus, to embark in this journey is to embody the divine, to touch the countless, and to simply come to be a co-creator with the universe.

Chapter 7: Emotional Intelligence

7.1. Defining Emotional Intelligence (EI) Understanding emotions and their effect.

Within the tapestry of human life, emotions stand as colourful threads, weaving together the fabric of our recollections, perceptions, and moves. These powerful forces, regularly seen as fleeting and ephemeral, shape our global in strategies each diffused and profound. Yet not all apprehend or understand the tough dance of feelings, and less nonetheless harness their whole capability. This reputation, knowledge, and subsequent mastery is what defines Emotional Intelligence.

At its middle, Emotional Intelligence is the functionality to be privy to, manage, and explicit one's feelings while dealing with interpersonal relationships judiciously and empathetically. But this definition, while concise, surely skims the floor of a depth this is massive and complex. Emotional Intelligence isn't always quite a fantastic deal recognizing one's very very very own emotions but moreover approximately discerning the emotions of others, distinguishing between one-of-a-type feelings, and the usage of this statistics to guide questioning and conduct.

Imagine repute at the edge of a big ocean. The waves, some mild and others fierce, represent our feelings. Some waves deliver with them treasures from the deep, at the identical time as others may supply particles. Just as one should apprehend the man or woman of these waves to navigate the waters properly, one want to apprehend and recognize feelings to navigate the complexities of existence. Emotional Intelligence, then, becomes the compass, the guiding big call, on this big ocean of feelings.

One may additionally ask, why is such statistics critical? To that, do not forget the function feelings play in every element of our lives. From the options we make, the relationships we foster, to the desires we pursue, emotions are the underlying currents. A preference made in anger differs extremely from one made in calm mirrored image. A verbal exchange had with empathy differs from one steeped in indifference. Every emotion, be it pleasure, sorrow, anger, or love, hues our notion and affects our actions.

However, it is not pretty lots recognizing those emotions. True Emotional Intelligence lies in the alchemy of remodeling them, of using them to one's gain. It is set taking the uncooked, frequently tumultuous electricity of feelings and channeling it toward fantastic ends. It is the art work of turning anger into ardour, sorrow into reflected photo, and pleasure into inspiration.

To the discerning man or woman, emotions additionally become a reflect, reflecting the innermost recesses of the thoughts and soul. They offer clues, hints approximately dreams, aspirations, fears, and desires. By information the ones symptoms, you may nevertheless align themselves more cautiously with their actual cause, developing a existence that resonates with authenticity and ardour.

Furthermore, in the realm of interpersonal relationships, Emotional Intelligence is the bridge that connects souls. It fosters expertise, creates bonds, and cultivates mutual recognize. An person attuned to the emotions of others can create harmonious relationships, every non-public and professional. They can revel in the unspoken, enjoy the underlying currents, and respond with understanding and care.

Yet, it is critical to notice that Emotional Intelligence is not a static trait however a dynamic skills. Like the muscle mass of the frame, it could be advanced, honed, and sensitive. Through mirrored image, mindfulness, and exercising, you can heighten their emotional reputation, decorate their capacity to control and harness emotions, and beautify their interpersonal competencies.

In a worldwide that regularly emphasizes highbrow prowess, Emotional Intelligence stands as a testament to the electricity of the coronary coronary coronary heart. It reminds us that actual understanding is not quite heaps facts but about understanding. It's no longer pretty lots questioning but feeling. And it's not just about man or woman achievement however approximately developing a international full of concord, expertise, and love.

To embark on the adventure of getting to know Emotional Intelligence is to embark on a quest for deeper knowledge, each of the self and of the arena. It is to apprehend the symphony of feelings that plays interior each coronary coronary heart and to turn out to be the conductor of this grand orchestra. It is to create a existence that is not absolutely lived however felt, a life wealthy in recollections, relationships, and profound data.

As you delve deeper into this realm, might also you find out the treasures that lie inside your emotional depths. May you understand the power and potential of each emotion and use them to craft a lifestyles of cause, passion, and profound connection. For, in the dance of feelings, lies the real essence of existence, ready to be located, understood, and loved.

7.2 Emotional Intelligence and Visualization: How Understanding Emotions Can Enhance Visualization.

Delving into the depths of 1's thoughts, one encounters a massive expanse in which imagination and emotion meld, creating colorful tapestries of idea and feeling. It is in this realm that the paintings of visualization thrives. But to virtually harness its potential, one need to recognize the tough dance amongst visualization and emotional intelligence.

Visualization is not honestly the act of conjuring snap shots in the mind. It is a profound technique, a adventure into the world of opportunity. Here, one paints pix of goals, aspirations, and desires. Yet, the ones pics benefit existence, vibrancy, and overall performance even as infused with the uncooked strength of emotion.

Think of a seed, brimming with capability. Alone, it stays dormant. But given the right conditions – fertile soil, water, daylight – it burgeons into a towering tree. Similarly, a visualization, even as nurtured with emotion, transforms from a trifling idea right right into a great pressure, capable of shaping fact.

Emotional intelligence, with its emphasis on knowledge, spotting, and dealing with feelings, becomes the guiding hand in this transformative system. By discerning the feelings that underpin a visualization, you may growth its energy, making it resonate more deeply inside the recesses of the subconscious.

Imagine visualizing a dream domestic. The structure, layout, and place might be smooth. Yet, even as one infuses this photograph with the feelings of satisfaction, safety, and pride related to proudly proudly proudly owning this form of haven, the visualization turns into more potent. It's now not only a residence; it's miles a sanctuary, a testament to at least one's achievements and aspirations.

Furthermore, emotional intelligence aids in navigating the capability pitfalls within the realm of visualization. Not all feelings that rise up are positive. Doubts, fears, and insecurities may additionally additionally cloud the intellectual photo, distorting it, or diminishing its vibrancy. Here, the capability to understand and manage the ones emotions will become vital. By acknowledging them and gently steerage the mind away, one guarantees that the visualization remains untainted and effective.

However, there may be an extremely good extra profound synergy among emotional intelligence and visualization. When one visualizes with readability and emotional intensity, the feelings generated act as a compass, guiding one inside the direction of the realization of that image. It's a magnetic pull, an unseen strain that draws reality in the direction of the visualized cause. The emotions felt throughout this machine become signals to the universe, communicating one's goals and intentions.

Let's delve deeper. The universe, in its endless awareness, responds no longer in fact to thoughts, but to the feelings that accompany them. A desire, even as paired with the emotion of unwavering belief, sends a more potent signal than an insignificant want. Emotional intelligence, through assisting inside the technology and control of those emotions, ensures that the indicators one sends are clear, steady, and compelling.

Moreover, the device of visualization will become a journey of self-discovery. As one delves into the feelings associated with their goals, they gain insights into their actual motivations, values, and priorities. It's an introspective voyage in which desires are not certainly seen however felt, and in that feeling lies the seed of their popularity.

Consider furthermore the ripple effects of this synergy within the realm of interpersonal relationships. When one visualizes effects in interactions with others, data the emotions worried - each one's very own and those of the other birthday party - can pave the way for harmonious exchanges. Envisioning a communique with a cherished one, and feeling the feelings of know-how, empathy, and love, can redesign that upcoming interplay, making it resonate with those very emotions.

In the grand tapestry of life, in which thoughts and feelings intertwine, the dance amongst emotional intelligence and visualization stands proud as a dance of creation. It's a harmonious ballet wherein information fuels creativeness, and emotions provide wings to desires.

So, as you embark on the adventure of visualization, permit your emotional intelligence be the wind on your sails. Recognize the power of your emotions, harness them, and infuse your visualizations with their energy. For on this union lies the vital factor to reworking the intangible nation-states of idea and emotion into tangible realities. Embrace this synergy, and watch because the area around you molds itself, echoing the desires of your coronary coronary heart and the aspirations of your soul.

7.Three. Cultivating Emotional Intelligence: Techniques and Practices.

Deep inside everyone lies an expanse of feelings, exquisite and varied, ready to be navigated. Much like a gardener tending to a garden, nurturing each plant with care and precision, we too should generally tend to our emotional landscapes. It is on this attentive cultivation that the mastery of Emotional Intelligence (EI) is birthed.

First and fundamental, the journey of cultivating EI requires the seeker to be an astute observer of oneself. Self-attention, the beacon that illuminates our emotional landscapes, lets in for the popularity of emotions as they upward push up. But how does one sharpen this intrinsic experience of interest? The answer lies inside the age-antique workout of mindfulness. By anchoring oneself inside the present moment, by means of manner of listening to the whispers of the coronary coronary heart and the murmurs of the thoughts, one becomes attuned to the ebb and drift in their emotional tides. This exercise, whether or now not done in quiet reflected picture or during the every day chores of existence, builds the muse of EI.

Building in this foundation, the artwork of emotional law turns into handy. Picture a sailor adjusting sails to the whims of the wind, making sure the boat remains steady and on direction. Similarly, with the knowledge of our feelings, we advantage the capacity to navigate them, making sure they serve us in place of dominate us. The workout of deep breathing, for instance, can be a profound device on this mission. When engulfed through an emotion, taking deep, measured breaths acts as an anchor, grounding one and allowing the emotion to be observed without being overtaken via the usage of it.

Yet, facts oneself is but one element of EI. Understanding others, empathizing with their emotional landscapes, is its dual pillar. To surely stroll a mile in every different's footwear, to revel in their delight, their pain, their hopes, and their fears, is a talent every noble and crucial. A easy approach to foster this is lively listening. By clearly immersing oneself in every different's terms, with the useful resource of putting apart judgments and preconceived notions, one opens the door to real information. In this attentive listening, emotions, often unstated, display themselves, granting insights into the coronary heart of the speaker.

Furthermore, the exercise of journaling can feature both a mirror and a map in the adventure of EI cultivation. By penning down one's thoughts and feelings, styles emerge. Emotions, as quick as nebulous, take shape, revealing triggers, reactions, and nuances.

Over time, this act of writing becomes a speak with oneself, imparting clarity, expertise, and knowledge. It is a vicinity in which emotions can be dissected, understood, and ultimately mastered.

Yet, even in this adventure of emotional mastery, annoying conditions will get up. Distractions, external impacts, societal norms, and internal biases can cloud judgment and prevent the cultivation of EI. Here, the workout of self-reflected photo turns into paramount. Setting apart moments inside the day, some distance from the hustle and bustle, to introspect on one's emotional responses and reactions, permits for direction correction. It's corresponding to a gardener pruning away the weeds, making sure the emotional garden stays lush and colourful.

To decorate this cultivation technique, surround oneself with environments and people that nurture emotional increase. Engaging in discussions, sharing emotional critiques, and looking for remarks can provide useful insights. After all, anyone is a totally specific repository of emotional studies, and through sharing, we beautify our information manifold.

In this voyage of emotional discovery, staying electricity is a relied on ally. Just as a seed, even as planted, requires time, nourishment, and care to blossom, so does the cultivation of EI. Celebrate the small victories, the moments of readability, the instances of deep empathy, and recognize them as milestones in this journey.

Remember the cultivation of Emotional Intelligence isn't always a holiday spot but a journey. A adventure that enriches, enlightens, and empowers. As you navigate the wonderful expanse of your emotional landscape, allow those techniques and practices be your guiding stars. For in studying one's feelings lies the vital thing to facts oneself, expertise others, and unlocking the doorways to a harmonious existence.

Chapter 8: Understanding Visualization

Visualization is a sturdy approach that taps into the innate ability of our minds to create awesome highbrow pix and scenes. In this bankruptcy, we can have a look at the because of this and idea of visualization, dig into the era behind its effectiveness, and evaluation specific varieties of visualization strategies.

2.1 Definition and Concept of Visualization

At its center, vision is the approach of the usage of our minds to create designated intellectual snap shots or fashions of precise conditions, sports, or supposed effects. By enticing our emotions and feelings in this intellectual exercise, we make the revel in more real and attractive.

Imagine yourself on a quiet beach, feeling the warm temperature of the solar, listening to the mild waves, and tasting the salty sea breeze. Visualization allows you have got interaction yourself completely in this highbrow global, bringing it to lifestyles as in case you were bodily there.

2.2. The Science behind Visualization and How It Affects the Brain

The success of imagery lies in its impact on the thoughts. Our brains are instead flexible, and that they do no longer constantly distinguish between actual and imagined sports. When we be given as actual with an motion or situation, the equal mind pathways are engaged as if we have been sincerely appearing that motion.

A neuroscience take a look at has validated that in vision, the mind's nerves fireside in patterns similar to those noticed for the duration of actual-life activities. This technique is called "neuroplasticity," in which the mind reshapes and rewires itself primarily based absolutely totally on repeated concept styles.

Moreover, creativeness triggers the discharge of hormones like dopamine and serotonin, which beautify power, consciousness, and glad feelings. These neurochemicals help the mind hyperlinks related to the imagined situation, making it more likely to be completed in fact.

2.Three Different Types of Visualization Techniques

There are numerous rendering techniques that cater to one among a type tastes and goals. Here are some famous ones:

Outcome Visualization:

Envisioning the a success achievement of your desires in outstanding element See your self gambling the achievement and feeling the feelings worried with it.

Sensory Visualization: Engaging all of your senses to create a multidimensional experience to your thoughts This can incorporate feeling textures, paying attention to sounds, smelling smells, and consuming tastes related to your photo.

Guided visualization: following a pre-recorded or written script that takes you on a adventure thru precise conditions meant to rouse super feelings and self-discovery.

Symbolic Visualization: Using pics or thoughts to provide an reason behind your dreams or obstacles This technique may be

mainly beneficial at the same time as picturing complicated thoughts.

5. Past Experience Visualization:

Revisiting a exceptional beyond revel in and repeating it in your thoughts This approach can growth self assurance and strength with the useful resource of reminding you of past successes.

6. Future Self-Visualization:

Imagining your self due to the fact the wonderful version of yourself inside the destiny Visualize the person you try to become and the life you need to manual.

2.Four Integrating Visualization into Your Self-Help Practice

As you begin for your imaginative and prescient journey, bear in thoughts that area and accept as true with inside the manner are key. Make time for normal practice and be affected individual with your self as you construct this skills.

In the imminent factors, we will dive deeper into specific imaginative and prescient sports and techniques for unique regions of self-help. Whether you're aiming for private increase, stress discount, or reason popularity, visualization is probably your relied on companion in turning your dreams into fact.

Now that you have a higher understanding of visualization's due to this, the technological information at the back of its effects at the thoughts, and the precise strategies to be had, it's time to dive into the real application of visualization for yourself-help journey. Let's launch the overall strength of your thoughts and set the degree for fantastic trade.

Setting Clear Goals for Visualization

In this monetary disaster, we are capable of look at the fee of putting clean and realistic dreams for imaginative and prescient. We'll dig into why reason placing is a critical part of the imaginative and prescient and provide you with a step-with the aid of manner of-step guide to describing your desires correctly.

3.1 The Significance of Setting Specific and Achievable Goals for Visualization

Visualizing with out clear goals is like placing sail without a area. To make the most of vision as a self-help device, it's miles crucial to have properly-described goals. Specific and practical desires supply route to your meditation exercise, ensuring that your efforts are focused and beneficial.

Setting particular desires allows your thoughts construct particular intellectual pix of what you want to reap. The extra shiny and particular your pictures, the greater effective their impact on your unconscious thoughts. It permits your thoughts spot opportunities and assets that in shape your photo, making it less difficult to create your goals.

Moreover, realistic goals create a sense of self assurance and strain. When your dreams are practical and feasible, you're more likely to just accept as real with on your capability to attain them. This notion promotes a top notch mind-set, allowing you to live committed to your visualization practice and take the essential actions to expose your goals into truth.

3.2 Step-with the useful resource of-Step Guide to Defining Your Goals Effectively

Follow these steps to create clean and practical dreams for visualisation:

Step 1: Self-Reflection

Take time to do not forget your life, goals, and locations in that you would like to appearance properly adjustments. Consider your lengthy-time period vision and damage it down into smaller, feasible desires.

Step 2: Specificity

Make your dreams as particular as feasible. Avoid vague terms like "I need to attain achievement" and rather describe what achievement way to you in particular phrases. For example, "I want to begin my non-public on-line business organisation and generate $10,000 in income inside the subsequent six months."

Step 3: Realism

Assess the opportunity of your desires. Are they feasible internal a sincere time frame? Setting faux dreams can bring about anger and demotivation. Aim immoderate, however be realistic about what you can advantage.

Step four: Write it down.

Document your goals in writing. Putting them on paper strengthens your pledge and makes them more actual. Use amazing words and provoking comments to useful resource your notion to your capability to gain them.

Step five: Visualize the final outcomes

Close your eyes and hold in mind your self effectively reaching each motive. See the records, sense the feelings, and enjoy the pride of success. Embrace the adventure and assume correct modifications alongside the manner.

Step 6: Create an Action Plan

Break down your dreams into smaller steps and make an motion plan. Outline the proper steps you want to take to move towards your goals. Celebrate each milestone as you boom.

Step 7: Review and adjust

Regularly evaluation your dreams and the paintings you have got got carried out. Adjust your meditation workout and motion plan as needed to stay heading within the proper course. Be bendy and open to changing your desires if times change.

Remember that purpose-putting and vision are converting processes. As you growth and evolve, your goals also can alternate too. Embrace the road of self-discovery, and use creativeness as a tool to influence you toward a greater appropriate life.

With clean and realistic dreams in area, you're now prepared to boost your meditation workout and make it an important part of your self-assist adventure. In the following financial break, we will have a look at a manner to construct the right highbrow putting to decorate the success of your workout. Let's maintain in this converting street together.

Chapter 9: Creating The Ideal Visualization Environment

In this monetary disaster, we are able to explore the importance of locating a non violent and distraction-unfastened vicinity for visualization and offer you with beneficial pointers to decorate the temper of your visualization practice. By developing a great putting, you could decorate the usefulness of your mind and enhance yourself-assist adventure.

4.1 How to Find a Calm and Distraction-Free Space for Visualization

Finding the right placing for visualisation is critical to assisting you completely have interaction yourself inside the practice and promote a deep sense of focus and rest. Follow those steps to find out a peaceful and distraction-loose area:

Step 1: Assess Your Surroundings

Look spherical your dwelling area and find out regions which is probably quiet and loose from outdoor noises. It might be a cushty area for your mattress room, a quiet spot in your out of doors, or any location wherein you could experience secure and non violent.

Step 2: Eliminate distractions

Clear your preferred region of any feasible interruptions. Put away digital gadgets, turn off signs, and restrict visible litter. The purpose is to create a setting that lets in you hobby absolutely to your meditation exercise.

Step three: Use headphones (optionally to be had)

If you live in a loud setting or percentage your dwelling region with others, strive using headphones within the course of your vision exercise. Noise-canceling headphones can assist create a bubble of calm, permitting you to reputation completely on your inner enjoy.

Step 4: Set Boundaries

Communicate with those round you approximately your vision workout and request their records and manual. Let them understand that in this time, you want quiet and minimal interruptions to make the maximum of your meetings.

four.2 Tips to Enhance the Ambiance of Your Visualization Practice

Once you have got discovered your calm and distraction-free location, bear in mind including the subsequent tips to enhance the temper of your meditation exercising:

Tip 1: Lighting

Choose easy, warmth lighting fixtures in your seen place. Dim the lights or use candles to create a relaxed and quiet environment. Avoid strong, brilliant lighting that might wreck your attention.

Tip 2: Aromatherapy

Consider using crucial oils or candles with relaxing smells like lavender, chamomile, or sandalwood. Aromatherapy can assist lighten up your thoughts and supply a lift for your quiet nation all through visualization.

Tip three: Comfortable Seating

Select a comfy chair, cushion, or mat to take a seat down on in the end of your visualization exercising. The greater snug your frame is, the much less tough it is to allow skip of physical strain and certainly interact in intellectual pictures.

Tip four: Background Music or Sounds

Soft historical past track or nature seems like mild rain, strolling water, or rustling leaves can enhance the mood of your imaginative and prescient area. These sounds can be soothing and help keep your interest.

Tip 5: Visualization Props Consider using: Visualization props like crystals, pics, or symbolic gadgets linked to your goals. These props can function recollections of your desires and add a bodily element to your exercise.

Tip 6: Time of Day

Choose a time of day that suits together at the side of your herbal rhythm and even as you are most cushty and conscious. For some, the morning is probably great for a clean start, on the equal time as others might also moreover pick nights for idea and visualization.

By developing welcoming and peaceful surroundings, you signal in your mind that it's time for a targeted meditation exercise. This setting gadgets the degree for a deeper and extra changing enjoy during each lesson.

In the next element, we are able to test numerous guided meditation responsibilities ideal to superb regions of self-help. These responsibilities will characteristic beneficial gear for your journey toward non-public growth and properly-being. Let's maintain this powerful test of photos strategies for self-help.

Guided Visualization Exercises for Self-Help

In this financial ruin, we are able to find out numerous guided visualization sports sports that may be effective equipment on your journey of self-help. These bodily activities are designed to help you reduce pressure, boom self assurance, beautify health, and further. Follow the ideal instructions and visualization scripts provided beneath to tap into the transformative potential of visualization.

5.1 Guided Visualization Exercise 1: Inner Sanctuary

Purpose: To create a mental sanctuary in which you may locate peace, rest, and rejuvenation.

Instructions:

Find a cushty seated or mendacity position for your calm and distraction-free visualization space.

Take some deep breaths to loosen up your frame and mind.

Close your eyes and recollect a lovable, serene vicinity in nature. It may be a beach, a wooded area, a meadow, or any location that brings you a feel of tranquility.

Visualize the records of this area—the colours, the sounds, and the scents. Engage all of your senses to make the enjoy as vibrant as possible.

As you discover your inner sanctuary, discover a gap in which you can take a seat down or lie all of the manner right down to rest.

Feel the slight warmth of the sun in your pores and pores and skin, the softness of the grass underneath you, and the peacefulness of the surroundings.

Stay on this sanctuary for so long as you want, soaking in its calming energy and recharging your spirit.

When you are prepared to go back, take some deep breaths and open your eyes, bringing the tranquility of your inner sanctuary with you into the winning second.

5.2 Guided Visualization Exercise 2: Confidence Booster

Purpose: To enhance self-self assure and self-perception via manner of visualizing a fulfillment accomplishments.

Instructions:

Sit or stand without problems on your visualization place.

Take a moment to recollect a past experience in that you felt assured and executed. It may be a a success presentation, a sports activities activities fulfillment, or any second that made you feel proud.

Close your eyes and vividly visualize that beyond enjoy. See yourself inside the situation, experience the emotions, and recall the outstanding comments and praise you received.

Allow the ones feelings of self belief and fulfillment to fill your whole being.

Imagine your self in a future state of affairs in that you want to feel assured. It is probably a undertaking interview, a social occasion, or any state of affairs that demanding situations your self-assure.

Visualize your self performing effects, grace, and self-guarantee. Embrace the same self assurance you felt within the beyond.

See your self receiving powerful responses and feeling satisfied along side your achievements.

Hold without delay to this empowering feeling of self assurance as you open your eyes, understanding that you have the capability to succeed in any scenario.

5.Three Guided Visualization Exercise 3: Healing and Wellness

Purpose: To promote bodily and intellectual well-being thru visualization.

Instructions:

Sit or lie down effortlessly for your visualization space.

Take a few deep breaths to lighten up your frame and mind.

Close your eyes and recognition to your breath, allowing any tension or pressure to soften away.

Now, visualize a restoration mild surrounding you. It may be any color that resonates with you—blue, inexperienced, or golden, for example.

See this restoration slight enveloping your complete body, bringing warm temperature and luxury to each cellular.

As the moderate permeates your body, visualize it dissolving any physical discomfort or illnesses you will be experiencing.

Feel the healing electricity restoring stability and harmony internal you.

Shift your attention on your intellectual properly-being. Visualize the healing mild clearing away any bad mind or feelings, making area for positivity and peace.

Stay on this recovery slight for so long as you need, information that you are nurturing your well-being on all degrees.

When you are organized, take a few deep breaths and open your eyes, feeling refreshed and rejuvenated.

By regularly practicing the ones guided visualization physical games, you could harness the transformative strength of visualization to help your self-assist adventure. Each exercise objectives precise regions of your existence, empowering you to create brilliant changes and foster personal boom. Use those visualization scripts as equipment to release your inner capability and manifest the lifestyles you preference.

In the following bankruptcy, we will discover the mixing of affirmations with visualization, combining their forces to growth your self-assist workout. Let's preserve our exploration of powerful visualization strategies for holistic properly-being and self-development.

Visualization and Affirmations: A Powerful Synergy

In this financial disaster, we are going to discover the dynamic synergy between visualization and great affirmations, growing a powerful combination for self-assist and private transformation. We'll delve into the art of crafting effective affirmations and offer steering on seamlessly integrating them into your visualization exercising.

6.1 Combining Positive Affirmations with Visualization for a More Powerful Impact

Positive affirmations are empowering statements that strengthen first rate beliefs and self-encouragement. When blended with visualization, they act as catalysts for alternate, in addition enhancing the transformative energy of each practices.

While visualization creates vivid highbrow photographs of your chosen consequences, affirmations offer the verbal reinforcement had to solidify the ones intellectual photographs. The repetition of excessive first rate affirmations at some point of visualization serves to rewire your unconscious thoughts, replacing self-proscribing beliefs with empowering and uplifting mind.

Affirmations supplement visualization by way of instilling self perception and resolution and aligning your conscious and unconscious minds within the path of your desires. The more you engage with those effective thoughts and pix, the more potent the effect for your mind, feelings, and movements. This combination fosters a effective thoughts-set that propels you beforehand to your adventure of self-help.

6.2 Crafting Effective Affirmations and Integrating Them into Your Practice

Follow those steps to create powerful affirmations and seamlessly combine them into your visualization exercise:

Step 1: Identify Your Goals

Define the precise areas of your lifestyles in that you want to enjoy extremely good modifications. Whether it's far improving self-self assure, accomplishing achievement for your career, or fostering better relationships, be clean about your dreams.

Step 2: Use incredible language.

Craft affirmations within the present traumatic and use nice language. For instance, as opposed to announcing, "I will triumph over stressful situations," say, "I am capable of overcoming worrying situations pretty absolutely."

Step three: Keep Them Personal

Make the affirmations private and massive to you. Tailor them to reflect your particular aspirations and values, making sure they resonate deeply along side your unconscious mind.

Step four: Be unique.

Address the particular elements you want to work on. Specific affirmations are more targeted and characteristic a greater impact to your thoughts. For example, "I am assured and assertive during conferences" is greater powerful than a standard affirmation like "I am assured."

Step 5: Practice each day

Incorporate affirmations into your each day habitual. Repeat them severa times all through your visualization periods and sooner or later of the day. Consistent repetition is fundamental to rewiring your subconscious mind.

Step 6: Engage Emotions

Infuse your affirmations with proper feelings. Feel the pleasure, pleasure, and determination related to carrying out your desires as you repeat the affirmations. Emotional engagement makes them extra effective.

Step 7: Visualize with Affirmations

As you visualize your preferred outcomes, comprise affirmations associated with those dreams. For example, in case you're visualizing profession success, encompass affirmations like "I am able to excelling in my career" or "Opportunities float to me effects."

Step 8: Believe and Affirm within the Now

As you combine visualization and affirmations, remember within the possibility of your dreams coming actual. Affirm as even though your desires are already manifesting in the gift 2d, reinforcing a strong enjoy of perception and expectation.

By integrating powerful affirmations with visualization, you create a harmonious and empowering workout that propels you within the path of your desires. Embrace the transformational ability of this synergy as you nurture a nice and growth-orientated thoughts-set.

In the following bankruptcy, we are capable of deal with common obstacles encountered at some point of visualization and offer strategies to overcome them. Let's maintain our adventure of self-improvement thru the strength of visualization and best affirmations.

Chapter 10: Overcoming Obstacles In Visualization

In this monetary disaster, we are capable of discover commonplace worrying situations confronted eventually of vision and provide powerful techniques to conquer them. Additionally, we are able to cover strategies to live targeted and stimulated throughout your imagery workout, ensuring normal growth on your self-assist journey.

7.1 Addressing Common Challenges Encountered During Visualization

Visualization, like each workout, may also moreover provide fantastic limitations which can prevent your boom. Understanding and handling those hurdles will assist you float via them greater successfully. Some commonplace troubles are:

Challenge 1: Distractions Solution: In a international whole of distractions, finding consciousness may be tough. Create a designated imaginative and prescient area this is unfastened from interruptions and noise. Consider the usage of headphones or calm track to drown out noise.

Challenge 2: Lack of Clarity Solution: If you discover it tough to photograph particular facts, workout frequently and be affected person with your self. Start with easy pictures and regularly add extra information as your creativity improves.

Challenge three: Restlessness or Impatience Solution:

Restlessness is ordinary, specifically in case you are new to meditation. Practice cognizance or deep respiratory strategies earlier than imagery to calm your mind. Trust the method and understand that success takes time.

Challenge four: Negative Thoughts Solution:

When bad thoughts seem during visualization, apprehend them without judgment and gently shift your interest another time for your great snap shots. Incorporate mantras to fight pessimism.

Challenge five: Inconsistent Practice Solution:

Consistency is excessive to getting the rewards of meditation. Schedule regular meditation bodily sports, although they may be short. Set notes or upload meditation in your daily exercising to preserve balance.

7.2 Strategies to Stay Focused and Motivated

Maintaining interest and power for your imaginative and prescient exercising is crucial for prolonged-term achievement. Here are a few strategies that will help you stay on course:

Strategy 1: Set easy intentions:

Define your dreams and plans earlier than each vision workout. Remind yourself why you're working towards imaginative and prescient and what you hope to accumulate. This readability will preserve you inspired and centered at some level inside the exercising.

Strategy 2: Visualization Log Maintain:

A visualization log to song your increase and research. Write approximately your mind, emotions, and any insights you examine. Reflecting to your journey will maintain you inspired and help you be aware kinds of trade.

Strategy 3: Visualization Partners or Groups:

Connect with like-minded folks that also are practising imagery. Share your memories, problems, and successes with every other. Having a assist device will encourage you and keep you accountable.

Strategy 4: Mix Up Your Visualizations:

Keep your visualization workout new and interesting by the usage of including one-of-a-type styles of pics. Explore guided visualizations and progressive visualization, or maybe strive picturing brilliant elements of your existence in separate conferences.

Strategy five: Celebrate Small Wins:

Acknowledge and revel in each milestone and success, regardless of how small. Recognizing your increase will enhance your energy and fuel your preference to keep the exercising.

Strategy 6: Practice Gratitude

End every meditation consultation with thank you. Express recognize for the risk to develop, take delivery of as actual with, and apprehend your desires. Gratitude promotes happiness and continues you inspired to hold yourself-assist journey.

By dealing with not unusual boundaries and adopting the ones strategies, you can create a satisfying and converting vision workout. Embrace the system with endurance and commitment, knowledge that each belief receives you one step towards the life you consider.

In the subsequent bankruptcy, we are able to have a examine imaginative and prescient strategies for particular parts of self-assist, together with better health, lowering pressure, and gaining achievement. Let's hold our adventure of private boom and energy through the electricity of creativeness.

Visualization for Health and Well-Being

In this bankruptcy, we are able to look at precise meditation techniques for promoting bodily and intellectual properly-being. Additionally, we can investigate case studies and success tales of humans who've professional incredible blessings from imagery in restoration.

8.1 Specific Visualization Techniques for Promoting Physical and Mental Well-Being

Visualization can be a useful device for boosting your big health and well-being. Here are some unique strategies you can add to your self-assist workout:

Technique 1: Healing Light Visualization:

Visualize a warmness, sparkling mild surrounding any areas of ache or contamination to your body. See this recovery slight exciting and recuperation the ones areas, bringing a feel of remedy and properly-being.

Technique 2: Breath Awareness Visualization:

Practice deep respiration on the equal time as picturing your breath as a calming, cleaning strain. With each breath, image recovery power getting into your body, and with each exhale, launch any stress or negativity.

Technique three: Immune System Boost Visualization:

Visualize your immune device as a sturdy navy of cells, effectively guarding your frame from any volatile attackers. See the ones cells strolling collectively to beautify your defensive tool.

Technique four: Stress Release Visualization:

Imagine your self in a quiet natural placing, together with a chilled beach or a non violent wooded vicinity. Visualize the concern leaving your body with each breath, replaced via way of a deep feeling of rest and calm.

8.2 Case Studies and Success Stories of Individuals Benefiting from Visualization in Healing Case Study 1: Sarah's Journey to Recovery

Sarah, a cancer affected person receiving treatment, felt frightened and harassed. She brought recuperation slight to her each day workout. Through regular exercise, Sarah said reduced worry, higher sleep, and improved wellknown properly-being. Her meditation exercise matched her clinical remedy and helped in her restoration journey.

Case Study 2: John's Confidence Transformation

John struggled with low self-self warranty, hurting his hobby growth. He introduced self belief-building intellectual exercises to his every day workout, supported with the useful resource of high-quality statements. Over time, John felt an exceptional shift in his self-belief, which brought about exquisite speeches and advanced process prospects.

Success Story 1: Mindful Meditation and Stress Reduction

Karen, a hectic employee, suffered from consistent worry and anxiety. She traditional focus meditation and imagery as a manner to control her strain. Over severa weeks of everyday workout, Karen expert reduced strain degrees, stepped forward hobby, and better emotional manage.

Success Story 2: Visualizing Athletic Success

Alex, a hopeful athlete, used imagery to beautify his potential. Before sports activities, he imagined himself performing ideal movements and attaining personal bests. This exercising now not fine boosted his self assurance but moreover advanced his bodily functionality.

Visualization is a versatile and sturdy device that helps modern day restoration practices and self-help techniques. These case research and fulfillment testimonies show the potential of images in boosting physical and highbrow well-being, accomplishing non-public increase, and enhancing the overall quality of existence.

In the following detail, we are capable of have a look at imaginative and prescient techniques for success and fulfillment, the use of the strength of your thoughts to create your desires and pastimes. Let's hold our have a test of powerful vision practices to guide a greater satisfied life.

Visualization for Success and Achievement

In this chapter, we will check how vision can enhance success in various areas of life, together with jobs and studies. Additionally, we are able to dive into the powerful practice of imagining success and wins to enhance self-self assure and push you towards your goals.

nine.1 How Visualization Can Improve Performance in Various Areas of Life

Visualization is a beneficial tool for reinforcing success in unique areas of life. Here are specific techniques wherein visualization could make a large effect:

In Career: Visualize yourself excelling on your gift device, without problems going through barriers, and getting awesome effects.

Use creativeness to prepare for critical speeches or interviews, imagining yourself giving a captivating everyday performance.

See yourself progressing in your paintings, taking on principal roles, and hitting new heights of fulfillment.

In instructors, visualize your self focused and worried within the direction of have a study periods, taking in records effortlessly.

Imagine yourself resultseasily acing exams and remembering records effectively.

Imagine incredible consequences for university tasks, speeches, and research.

In sports activities activities sports, use visualization to decorate physical performance through picturing best movements and terrific results.

See yourself conquering hurdles and going beyond limits to accumulate sports sports dreams.

Visualize being in a rustic of glide and pinnacle fulfillment all through events.

Personal Goals: Visualize the successful very last touch of personal desires, together with analyzing a modern expertise, beginning a business enterprise, or taking region a health revel in.

Imagine a healthful and glad life wherein your personal and artwork dreams flawlessly in shape.

9.2 Visualizing Success and Accomplishments to Boost Self-Confidence

Visualization is a robust device for building self-self notion and growing a success-orientated thoughts-set. Here's how you can use imagination to beautify self-self guarantee:

Step 1: Set smooth dreams.

Define tremendous dreams that match your goals. The more thorough your dreams are, the much less complicated it's far to anticipate and create them.

Step 2: Create bright visualizations.

Close your eyes and certainly image yourself accomplishing every cause. Engage all of your senses and experience the feelings worried collectively at the side of your success.

Step three: Embrace Positive Emotions:

As you don't forget your successes, enjoy the satisfaction, pride, and happiness that encompass accomplishing your desires. Embrace those nicely emotions absolutely.

Step four: Practice frequently:

Consistent imagery improves the thoughts pathways associated with success and self-self notion. Make imagery a each day exercising to boost the ones properly thoughts.

Step five: Use affirmations:

Incorporate mantras that healthful your imagined success. Repeat tremendous terms that manual your self-self notion and remember in your talents.

Chapter 11: Visualization For Personal Growth

In this financial disaster, we will discover how visualization may be a effective device for non-public increase and self-discovery. By mastering the electricity of your thoughts, you may start on a journey of self-improvement, find out thriller capacity, and make bigger better facts of yourself.

10.1 Exploring Personal Growth Through Visualization

Visualization performs a vital position in private boom, imparting a course to self-recognition and self-empowerment. Here are tactics to apply imagination for non-public increase:

Self-Awareness: Visualize times of self-reflection wherein you examine your abilties, flaws, and ideals. By information your self better, you could make informed options and healthy your behaviors alongside aspect your true self.

Positive Belief System: Use imagery to replace self-limiting thoughts with excessive incredible statements. Visualize your self accepting new mind that help your increase and ability.

Embracing Change: Visualize your self boldly shifting through life's adjustments and difficulties. This exercise cultivates grit and versatility, permitting you to simply accept boom possibilities.

Goal Manifestation:

Use your creativeness to look your self engaging in your goals. Visualizing fulfillment strengthens your willpower and power to take the critical steps closer to your goals.

10.2 Using Visualization as a Tool for Self-Discovery and Self-Improvement

Visualization is a course to self-discovery, liberating thriller elements of your self, and sparking personal increase. Here's a way to apply imagery as a tool for self-development:

Creative Exploration: Visualize your self engaged in innovative duties, which incorporates writing, drawing, or playing track. Allow your mind to float with out problem, encouraging creativity and self-expression.

Inner communication: During meditation, interact in an inner verbal exchange with your self. Ask questions and listen in your internal records for thoughts and path.

Exploring pursuits: Visualize yourself following your pastimes and hobbies. This exercise links you together with your actual pursuits and feeds your pleasure for lifestyles.

Uncovering Fears: Confront Your Fears Through Imagery See yourself conquering limitations, accepting weak point, and shifting out of doors your consolation place.

Imagery Meditation: Use imagery as a shape of meditation, going deep into your internal international and exploring your mind and emotions without judgment.

Self-Compassion: Visualize times of self-compassion and self-love. Embrace your self with love and information, developing a wholesome and satisfied self-image.

As you discover self-discovery through imagery, be open to insights and achieve all components of your self. Visualization can be a powerful device for personal exchange, permitting you to hook up with your real self and construct a existence related for your values and dreams.

In Conclusion

Visualization is a flexible and effective tool for non-public boom, self-discovery, and self-improvement. Throughout this e-book, we've studied numerous drawing strategies and their makes use of in remarkable areas of existence.

Remember that meditation is a workout that dreams consistency and endurance. As you boom this expertise, be moderate with yourself and allow the method to unfold obviously. Visualization is a lifelong way of self-recognition and power, moving you inside the direction of a extra gratifying and richer life.

Embrace the energy of your thoughts, believe to your functionality to create incredible modifications, and preserve to harness the converting functionality of imagery in your self-help adventure.

Now, armed with the facts and system given in this ebook, it is time to begin to your drawing adventure. May your avenue be whole of increase, self-discovery, and happiness. Happy wondering!

Visualization for Stress Relief and Inner Peace

In this chapter, we can test strategies to apply creativeness to alleviate fear and promote relaxation. Additionally, we're going to dive into particular meditation workouts purported to encourage calmness and increase inner peace.

eleven.1 Techniques for Using Visualization to Alleviate Stress and Promote Relaxation

Visualization can be a strong tool to overcome stress and promote relaxation.

Here are some techniques to help you manipulate strain efficiently:

Nature Retreat Visualization: Close your eyes and remember yourself in a non violent nature placing, together with a tranquil seaside, a serene wooded region, or a relaxing park. Engage your senses to make the imaginative and prescient revel in as severe as feasible, feeling the calming breeze, paying attention to the slight rustling of leaves, and smelling the fragrance of nature. Spend time on this intellectual hideaway to permit pass of pressure and enjoy actual relaxation.

Breathing Visualization: Practice deep breathing at the identical time as picturing your breath as a moving float of calming power. With each inhale, photograph renewing power getting into your frame, and with each exhale, release tightness and fear. Focus on the flow of your breath and use this photo to discover a feeling of internal calm.

Balloon Release Visualization: Imagine pressure and lousy feelings as balloons tied in your wrist. Visualize yourself launching those balloons one by one into the sky, looking them waft away until the sky is obvious and unfastened from duties. As you drop each bubble, experience the burden of worry and tightness depart your body, making place for peace and calm.

11.2 Visualization Exercises to Induce Calmness and Inner Peace

Visualization may be a effective tool to boom inner peace and a sense of calm.

Here are particular duties to create peace and serenity:

Candle Flame Visualization: Picture a swirling candle flame in your head. Focus on the moderate movement of the mild and the adore it radiates. As you popularity at the mild, allow any dashing mind to subside, leaving you in a country of peaceful silence.

Lake Reflection Visualization: Imagine a quiet lake with although waves. Imagine your self sitting by manner of the shore, watching the picture of the surrounding beauty on the calm water's floor. As you watch the non violent image, permit your mind settle proper right into a country of inner peace.

Cloud Drifting Visualization: Imagine yourself lying on your lower again, looking up on the sky full of soft clouds. Visualize the clouds slowly shifting at a few stage within the sky, representing the passing nature of mind and fears. Let skip of any issues and without a doubt be gift in the non violent 2d.

By regularly appearing intellectual sports activities for pressure release and internal peace, you may create a sturdy mindset that lets in you to cope with existence's boundaries with extra ease. Visualization allows you to create your intellectual haven, in which you could discover comfort, rest, and a renewed experience of stability.

In Conclusion,

Visualization is a versatile and powerful practice that improves various additives of existence. From self-improvement to pressure launch, the strength of your mind can free up the door to a extra exquisite and peaceful existence.

As you hold your visualizing journey, endure in thoughts that continuity and purpose are essential. Embrace every meditation exercising with an open coronary heart, and permit the high-quality electricity it produces effect each part of your being.

May your meditation exercise lead you to a lifestyles of harmony, well-being, and inner peace. Let the converting energy of creativeness lead you closer to a higher and greater gratifying future. Happy thinking!

Chapter 12: Integrating Visualization Into Your Daily Routine

In this bankruptcy, we're capable of explore useful recommendations for consisting of imagination results on your routine. Additionally, we are able to cover the significance of retaining a everyday exercising to reap prolonged-term consequences and maximize the blessings of images.

12.1 Tips for Incorporating Visualization Seamlessly into Your Routine

Integrating imagery into your every day routine allow you to make the maximum of its changing electricity.

Here are some recommendations to with out problem encompass visualization on your each day life:

Morning vision: Start your day with a brief vision exercising. Spend a couple of minutes picturing your dreams, placing first-rate plans for the day in advance, and building a nice mind-set that will help you via the worrying conditions and possibilities that could rise up.

Visualization Before Sleep: Use visualization as a part of your middle of the night exercise. Spend a few minutes earlier than sleep imagining accurate results and memories. This exercising can help you input a rustic of relaxation and sell deep sleep.

Visualization Breaks: Take short visualization breaks all through the day. When you enjoy exhausted or concerned, near your eyes for a couple of minutes and keep in mind a non violent scene or an super quit result. These quick intellectual breaks can refresh your thoughts and decorate attention.

Visualization diary: Keep a visualization diary to music your growth and memories. Write approximately your thoughts, the feelings you skilled, and any insights you obtained. The diary acts as a useful tool for concept and growth.

Visualization Partners or Groups:

Connect with others who workout imagery. Join a visualization institution or discover a visualization buddy to percentage evaluations and help every extraordinary in your travels.

Visualization with Other Practices:

Combine imagery with unique cognizance practices, together with meditation, yoga, or gratitude bodily sports. The connection amongst the ones sports can make more potent yourself-attention and improve private increase.

Visualization Props: Use actual things associated with your mind. Keep symbols, photographs, or vision forums reflecting your desires in your property or place of job to remind you of your dreams and keep you centered.

12.2 Maintaining a Consistent Practice for Lasting Results

Consistency is top to unlocking the entire functionality of pix. Here are techniques to hold a normal exercise going for lengthy-term outcomes:

Set a time table: Schedule a designated time for visualisation to your every day or weekly exercising. Treat it as an essential meeting with your self and commit to showing up regularly.

Start Small: If you're new to imagery, start with shorter instructions and often boom the period as you switch out to be greater snug. Consistent quick commands are more effective than random long durations.

Use reminders: set notes in your cellular telephone or use visible cues to prompt your meditation exercise. Associating imaginative and prescient with particular cues permits create a addiction.

Celebrate Progress: Celebrate the development you are making on your meditation workout. Acknowledge your willpower and any effective adjustments you word in your thinking and behaviors.

Be Patient and Kind to Yourself: Understand that growth may additionally furthermore take time, and balance is a machine of self-discovery. Be affected character and kind to yourself in the direction of the manner.

Adapt to Your Lifestyle: Make your vision bendy to fit your way of existence. If your schedule is busy, discover modern ways to add visualization into your recurring, even though it's a brief concept all through your each day pressure.

Focus at the Experience: Embrace the course of vision in preference to actually focusing at the consequences. Enjoy the approach of self-exploration and private growth.

By adding meditation effects in your routine and retaining a consistent exercising, you may loose up the total functionality of this effective tool. Visualization becomes an critical a part of yourself-assist adventure, essential you toward a extra exceptional and useful lifestyles.

In Conclusion,

Visualization is a strong and bendy device that lets in you to make accurate changes in every a part of your lifestyles. By which include visualization effortlessly for your everyday and jogging closer to often, you could tap into the entire capability of this method for lasting results.

As you continue to discover the converting power of pictures, keep in mind that the adventure is particular to you. Embrace every photo with an open coronary heart, and allow the pleasant electricity it produces to inspire your mind, emotions, and actions.

May your imagination stay a leading slight to your direction of personal boom and self-discovery. Let the changing strength of vision lead you toward a existence packed with that means, nicely-being, and electricity. Happy thinking!

Advanced Visualization Techniques and Precautions

In this chapter, we are in a position to check superior imaginative and prescient methods, inclusive of cutting-edge visualization and lucid goals. These techniques provide specific probabilities for self-discovery and private growth. However, additionally they require care and course to make sure regular and effective workout

13.1 Exploring Advanced Visualization Methods

Creative Visualization:

Creative visualization takes modern-day visualization a step similarly via attractive your mind to construct targeted scenes and reviews. In this approach, you actively take part in growing the photo, filling it with modern elements and sharp sensory information. Creative vision allows you to discover countless alternatives and create your needs thru the strength of your mind.

Lucid Dreaming:

Lucid dreaming is a rustic in which you come to be aware that you are dreaming whilst even though within the dream. In this heightened nation of focus, you could actively affect and direct the dream's development. Lucid dreaming offers a deep danger for discovery, hassle-solving, and intellectual healing within the dream worldwide.

thirteen.2 Precautions and Guidance for Practicing Advanced Techniques

While advanced visualization strategies may be sturdy system for personal increase, further they require precise steps to make sure a steady and glad enjoy. Here are some recommendations for reading complicated drawing techniques:

Develop a stable foundation:

Before reading advanced strategies, create a regular exercising of wellknown imagery. Strengthening your potential to awareness, loosen up, and take into account correctly will offer a robust base for the more complicated parts of superior visualization.

Seek records and steering:

Educate your self about innovative imagery and lucid dreaming through dependable assets. Books, commands, or guided meditation films can provide beneficial insights and strategies. Seeking recommendation from skilled practitioners can provide essential help and make sure that you method these strategies with knowledge and recognize.

Practice mindfulness and self-popularity:

Cultivate reputation and self-hobby to your every day existence. Advanced imagery strategies demand heightened popularity and manipulate over your thoughts and emotions. Regular popularity sports activities activities, at the side of yoga, can beautify your potential to stay present and targeted.

Set smooth dreams: Before trying revolutionary imaginative and prescient or lucid dreaming, set clean goals on your exercising. Be aware of the dreams you want to gather and the feasible areas of observe inside your thoughts. Setting appropriate and beneficial desires will guide your studies in a beneficial way.

Establish a secure surroundings:

For aware desires, make sure you have got have been given a safe and cushty sleep setting. Create a chilled sleep exercising that supports clarity. For innovative imagery, find out a quiet and non violent region wherein you can recognition without interruption.

Practice recognize and ethics:

Approach complicated pix with appreciate and ethical idea. Focus on inner improvement, healing, and studying in desire to the use of those techniques for awful goals. Respecting the limits of your very personal mind and the dream international is vital for a remarkable enjoy.

Embrace Self-Care: As with any meditation exercise, self-care is important. Ensure you get enough sleep, preserve a healthful manner of existence, and take breaks whilst favored. Engage in self-compassion and self-mirrored photograph inside the route of your superior imagery course.

Conclusion

Advanced imagery strategies offer particular opportunities for personal growth and have a look at in the worlds of imagination and the inner thoughts. As you journey into the arena of modern imagery and lucid desires, preserve in thoughts the price of making plans, know-how, and respect.

By performing those strategies cautiously and with caution, you could unencumber new stages of self-discovery, healing, and exchange. Embrace these superior imagery strategies as system to broaden your recognition and create a greater enjoyable and powerful lifestyles. Happy looking!

Chapter 13: Visualization And Manifestation

In this financial disaster, we are able to test the strong hyperlink amongst creativeness and reaching your dreams. We'll dive into how imagination may be a spark for bringing your wants to life. Additionally, we are able to percent real-existence times of people who've completed their goals via the exercise of pics.

14.1 Understanding the Connection Between Visualization and Manifesting Your Desires

Visualization is a important tool for growing your goals and turning your desires into truth. The technique of imaginative and prescient consists of using your mind to sincerely see, revel in, and enjoy your desires as even though they're already taking location in the gift second. The link amongst vision and creation lies inside the following aspects:

Conscious Focus: Visualization focuses your conscious thoughts on your desires and dreams. By constantly having high first rate pix and emotions to your thoughts, you ship clean messages for your unconscious, which performs a exquisite position in forming your beliefs and actions.

Alignment of Thoughts and Emotions: Visualization suits your thoughts and feelings at the side of your dreams. When your mind and feelings are in stability, you create a strong and unified electricity that draws comparable stories and possibilities.

Law of Attraction: The law of attraction says that like attracts like. When you believe your desires with happiness and belief, you magnetically draw similar power and times into your life, developing the possibility of accomplishing your needs.

Inspired Action: Visualization sparks stimulated motion. As you certainly picture your goals, you emerge as more aware of the stairs and actions vital to advantage them. Visualization drives idea and pushes you towards taking the critical steps to reveal your desires into fact.

14.2 Real-Life Examples of Individuals Achieving Their Dreams Through Visualization

Real-lifestyles fulfillment memories show the converting electricity of imagination in making desires a reality.

Here are amazing examples:

Example 1: Sara's Entrepreneurial Success:

Sara perception of beginning her private green clothing logo. Through vision, she observed herself developing sustainable garments, having a a success commercial enterprise, and having an superb effect at the fashion business enterprise. With everyday vision and focused attempt, Sara became her dream into fact. Her logo earned respect for its social strategies, and she or he or he have come to be an critical man or woman in the sustainable style network.

Example 2: Alex's Athletic Achievement:

Alex desired to turn out to be a competitive wrestler. He used imagery to peer himself preventing at the pinnacle diploma, achieving personal bests, and triumphing titles. With willpower and imaginative and prescient, Alex became his dreams into fact. He earned an opening on the country wide team and received numerous critical occasions, becoming a function version for younger gamers.

These real-life examples show how drawing can be a effective tool for changing desires into realistic successes. When paired with focused attempt, notion, and perseverance, imagery allows people to acquire their dreams and create the existence they believe.

Conclusion

Visualization is a effective pressure that fills the distance among thoughts and reality. By the usage of your mind to appearance and revel in your goals as already finished, you cause the powerful method of advent. Visualization fits your thoughts, emotions, and movements, drawing right reviews and probabilities into your lifestyles.

The real-lifestyles achievement recollections shared here function inspiring memories of the converting capability of pics. Embrace this workout as a manner to create a extra alluring and beneficial life. Let the strength of vision fuel your goals, and can you bravely create your needs and attain your desires. Happy developing!

Embracing Visualization for Ongoing Self-Improvement

In this very last financial break, we are able to evaluation the crucial aspect factors and takeaways from the ebook and offer aid to preserve the exercise of visualization for ongoing self-improvement.

15.1 Recap of Key Points and Takeaways

Throughout this ebook, we've studied the converting energy of imagination as a device for self-assist and personal growth. Here are the essential element elements and takeaways:

Visualization Defined: Visualization is the machine of the usage of your thoughts to create highbrow pix and stories that in form your goals and desires.

The Science Behind Visualization: Visualization stimulates unique components of the thoughts, affecting wondering strategies, stress, and behavior. Regular exercise improves mind pathways related to fulfillment.

Types of Visualization Techniques: We studied superb visualization strategies, which incorporates directed visualization, modern visualization, and restoration moderate visualization, amongst others.

Goal Setting and Visualization: Setting precise and sensible goals before imagery improves its usefulness and affords course to your experience.

Creating the Right Environment: Finding a snug and distraction-free vicinity improves the notable of your meditation exercise.

Enhancing the putting with calming elements improves the revel in.

Visualization for Various Purposes: We included visualization strategies for stress release, self-confidence, bodily and intellectual well-being, success, and self-discovery.

Combining Visualization with Positive Affirmations:

Integrating high-quality affirmations will boom the effect of visualization, selling constructive views and attitudes.

Addressing Challenges: We reviewed common hurdles in imagery and provided strategies to live centered and stimulated.

Advanced Visualization Techniques: Creative visualization and lucid desires provide specific probabilities for self-exploration and alternate.

Manifestation through Visualization: Visualization connects thoughts, emotions, and actions, developing the strength crucial to create dreams and obtain dreams.

15.2 Encouragement to Continue the Practice of Visualization

As you achieve the prevent of this e-book, we encourage you to hold the exercising of visualization for persisted self-improvement and personal increase. Visualization is a adventure of power and alternate, and its advantages develop with regular exercising.

Remember those vital elements as you keep your vision adventure:

Be affected character and continual: Visualization is a talent that grows over time. Be patient with yourself and stay chronic in your exercising, regardless of the truth that the results may not be right away.

Embrace Self-Discovery: Visualization opens the door to self-discovery. Embrace the thoughts and discoveries that come from coming across your inner worldwide.

Set Meaningful Intentions: Set clean and essential goals to your meditation exercise. Allow your desires and goals that will help you in this journey.

Enjoy Your Progress: Acknowledge and revel in your improvement, irrespective of how small. Each jump ahead is a evidence of your dedication to non-public growth.

Combine Visualization with Action: Visualization is a strong tool; however it isn't a opportunity for motion. Combine meditation with revolutionary motion to push yourself inside the path of your goals.

Be open to wealth: Visualization allows you tap into the wealth of the world. Embrace the notion that you are worth of all the success, happiness, and satisfaction that existence has to provide.

Chapter 14: Associative Technique

The associative method, additionally known as the mnemonic approach, is a way used to decorate reminiscence with the useful resource of associating new information with cutting-edge statistics or innovative or weird snap shots because of the fact the thoughts remembers unusual memories for an prolonged duration. By usi8ng this method, you may beautify your capability to memorize something.

Here are a few commonplace associative strategies used for memorization:

Create a phrase or word the use of the primary letter of each item you want to undergo in thoughts. For instance, to endure in thoughts the order of the planets (Mercury, Venus, Earth, Mars, Jupiter, Saturn, Uranus, Neptune), you can use the acronym "My Very Educated Mother Just Served Us Noodles" (M-V-E-M-J-S-U-N).

Visual imagery

Create intellectual photographs which accomplice the statistics you need to hold in thoughts with familiar or unusual items, places, or situations. It is simpler to memorize if the photo is extra outrageous or memorable. For instance, if you need to consider a buying list which incorporates eggs, milk, bread, and oranges, you might imagine yourself juggling eggs at the same time as swimming in a pool of milk, with slices of bread floating spherical you, and oranges bouncing on the diving board.

Method of loci

Visualize familiar vicinity like your home or a course you recognize properly. Associate each item you need to don't forget with a particular location in that area. When you need to bear in mind the facts, mentally stroll thru the familiar location and visualize the associated items in their respective locations.

Storytelling

Create a story which includes the statistics you need to take into account. The tale have to be interesting, attractive and noteworthy, linking the all objects collectively in a logical collection. As you recollect the story, you could don't forget the associated statistics.

Rhymes and songs

Convert the facts you want to preserve in thoughts right into a catchy rhyme or tune. The rhythm and melody could make the data greater memorable and much less difficult to recall every time you need to don't forget them.

Following are some lists of 20 gadgets every. Read aloud each gadgets call, close to your eyes and create a seen image of the objects associating with any extra-regular item like a flying fish with huge wings or a monkey the usage of on a dinosaur or someone having a snake round his neck. There is not any restrict to what picture you create, the simplest necessities being the image want to be a few thing unusual.

Exercise-1

Coffee mug

Bicycle

Sunglasses

Bookshelf

Tennis racket

Umbrella

Laptop

Camera

Backpack

Wristwatch

Water bottle

Guitar

Pillow

Pencil sharpener

Chess set

Alarm clock

Toothbrush

Picture frame

Headphones

Soccer ball

You are mentioned amongst your family individuals and friends for uncommon adventures and eccentricity. One sunny morning, at the same time as you've got been sipping espresso from a coffee mug fashioned like a dancing penguin. After ingesting espresso, you have been a lot entire of energy which you decided to go on an adventure ride.

You jumped on your bicycle and commenced out biking through the city, carrying more than one outsized shades which made all of us laugh at you as speedy as they located you. But you in all likelihood did not care approximately every person and persisted cycling.

You stopped at a library and went inner in that you stumbled upon a bookshelf which changed into hidden in a secret passage. With a mischievous smile to your lips, you pushed the bookshelf aside, and positioned a hidden chamber packed with sparkling tennis rackets of many sizes.

You had been given very curios and couldn't face up to choosing up one of the rackets. Filled with pride, you started swinging the racket around. While swinging the racket you by using manner of coincidence knocked over an umbrella stand, inflicting a colourful umbrellas to open up all round you. It have end up a sight that had every person within the library bursting into laughter.

But your journey turn out to be a ways from over. You hopped once more for your bicycle and pedaled to a nearby café, in which you located a hard and fast of buddies busy with gambling video video games on their laptops. You took out your polarized virtual digicam from your rabbit format backpack and secretly began taking pictures of your buddies with funny and uncommon expressions on their faces even as they have been playing the sport .

You stuffed your backpack with the pix you've got were given taken and started out your adventures adventure once more. As you have got been cycling, you observed a group of surely white dressed human beings with horrifying mask gathered in a park for a yoga consultation. You mingled with the gang, you stolen their diamond wristwatches and filled for your again p.C. Then began going for walks a long way from there.

When the session ended, simply everybody end up taken aback to discover someone stolen their diamond watches, and found that it became you. All of them commenced out taking walks at the back of your bicycle. They have been having huge sized water bottle in their hand which they used as water cannon and have been seeking to shoot you with the water jet. You began out eating water from all of the water jets and used the water as water cannon on them to throw them again to the park.

Amidst the chaos and laughter, you stored cycling and after going in advance you located a nearby zoo park in which a guitarist changed into gambling a lively song alongside together with his 12 ft height Guitar. For playing one-of-a-kind tunes, the guitarist saved jumping and playing the guitar. The rhythm compelled you to enroll in in, and soon you each began growing spontaneous melodies filling the park and all the human beings and animals of the park started out dancing.

The laughter endured as you've got got come to be very tired and collapsed onto the ground. You preferred to have a few relaxation. Looking at you, a purple colored rabbit came taking walks to you and pushed a big size pillow under your head. After having some rest, you went at once to visit the relaxation of the park. In a corner of the park, there has been large period pencil sharpener and all the animals have been sprucing sticks collected from the park, reworking them into shielding tools.

Very astonished with the resource of this gear production, you regarded spherical and determined a sensible owl sitting in hollow nest in close by tree and looking all of the paintings of sharpening gadget. You asked the owl about why those gear were being sharpened.

The owl knowledgeable you that a few human beings who have been gambling chess were not human however devils. After the nights descend, they redecorate into their real shape and try and kill animals and consume them.

You glanced carefully at their chess set and located that the chess set quantities contained particular shape of devils in choice to the ordinary portions. As you glanced at them, you caught their interest and all of then grew to end up their head inside the route of you. Their eyes have been burning with flames, they stared at you and invited you to join their recreation. The owl warned you about being cautious.

You gladly commonplace their provide to play chess and brought a comical twist through the use of the sharpened sticks as chess pieces, making the game hilariously unpredictable, all of them seemed harassed and scratched their heads.

Time flew by means of manner of, and because of the truth the sun began placing, an alarm clock hidden within the park's wood went off, startling anybody,. You were amused thru the unexpected wake-up and take-heed call that it come to be time to transport from there. You fake going to a nearby restroom to smooth up. There, you placed an deserted toothbrush and could not resist the use of it to comb your teeth, although it wasn't your brush. To your marvel all of your enamel have come to be very healthy and vibrant illuminating the park.

With a refreshed smile, you went out of the park and resumed your journey. At a ways, you decided a picturesque spot and could resist taking pictures it. You positioned a discarded photo body nearby, that you picked up and used as a makeshift camera frame, pretending to seize the scenery.

After capturing the environment, you couldn't face up to temptation to spend a while on this lovely location. You laid down at the grass and used more than one colourful headphones, which modified into proficient to you by way of the use of the usage of your lady buddy for listening your preferred music.

While resting you noticed on the moon and located that few astronauts had been playing soccer with a football ball which has multi colored LED lighting fixtures on its floor. One of the astronauts kicked the ball so difficult that it fell at the floor close to you. As you have been entire of electricity, you started out gambling football ball on my own and hit the ball to a cave wherein lived a lion. As the ball went internal, the lion roared and also you started on foot from there collectively with your bicycle paddling it as fast as you may.

You stopped only whilst you reached home. This changed into one of the maximum adventures days of your life which you can in no manner forget about.

Exercise-2

Forest

Church

Watermelon

Chair

Elephant

Ring

Tom Cruise

Water Tank

River

Camel

Moon

Cricket

Lion

Michel Jackson

Apple

Horse

Sea

Laptop

Bike

Shoes

You have been journeying on a frightening night time time time through a dense wooded vicinity and will listen the sounds of tress swaying and wing blowing on the equal time as all of a surprising your automobile stopped. You attempted to restart the auto severa times but could not be triumphant.

You had been no longer capable of determine to what to do and all at once you heard loud track. You grew to come to be your head toward the route of track and you observed that some far off location modified into glowing with colorful lighting fixtures. Curiously, you started strolling within the direction of the lights. When you reached there you have been surprised to see a adorable church in which a wedding rite changed into occurring.

When you reached close to the church, you made a decision that watermelon turned into served as food and all the animals were playing watermelon. You additionally picked up a big size watermelon as you have been very hungry. You sat on a chair and started out ingesting watermelon.

Suddenly an elephant came within the once more of you and pushed your chair along collectively with his big trunk. You fell down from chair, and the watermelon damaged into portions. But you were no longer worried approximately the watermelon as you misplaced your ring which modified into gifted with the useful resource of your female pal.

While searching your ring, you found Tom Cruise's touchdown near you. Tom Cruise came walking to you and requested "are you looking for this" and showed a hoop finger. You jumped on him in satisfaction, thanked him and asked – " in which did you get it?".

Tom Cruise informed you that he found the hoop near a huge water tank. Curiously, you asked him to show the water tank. He took you to the water tank which turn out to be near a big river.

There had been many white camels with wings, under the water tank. They were flying and taking human beings to the Moon experience. You jumped on a camel and started flying in the direction of Moon.

When you reached Moon, you made a decision that a cricket in form changed into going to begin and a Lion modified into prepared for batting.

Michel Jackson became the bowler and he began doing moon walk for bowling. To your wonder, he held an yellow apple in his hand in preference to a ball. When Michel Jackson changed into moon walking for bowling, a horse came jogging and he ate the apple. The crowd started out out laughing and throwing rotten eggs and tomatoes to the floor.

You jumped on the pony and started out out out the usage of. The horse took you to the earth over again and dropped you on a Sea shore. You have been amazed to look that many laptops have been swimming and jumping in the sea just like dolphins.

Suddenly, one pc jumped very high and landed close to you. Curiously, you switched at the laptop and started out playing a racing pastime of motorcycles. You desired that you could have this form of powerful bike. Your need become fulfilled and a powerful motorcycle seemed inside the front of you.

You jumped on the motorbike and commenced out the engine. Again you have got been amazed to peer that your cloths converted to the usage of healthy with helmet and colorful racing footwear. You kicked the motorbike and got here again home

Exercise-3

Telescope

Cookie jar

Cherry

Paintbrush

Cactus

Socks

Binoculars

Skipping rope

Fishing rod

Tape degree

Flower vase

Rubik's Cube

Skateboard

T-shirt

Calculator

Kitchen knife

Dumbbell

Alarm machine

Globe

Professor Gizmo changed into mentioned for his unusual creations and experiments. One day, he determined to combine his love for invention alongside alongside along with his ardour for cookies.

Using his telescope, Professor Gizmo observed planet made absolutely of cookies. Determined to supply the cookies in the world, he positioned a massive cookie jar on his rocket and released himself into place.

While floating inside the vicinity, Professor Gizmo observed a cluster of cherries floating weightlessly. He commenced out consuming cherries till he changed into truly satisfied.

When he changed into exciting in his rocket, sipping a cup of region tea, Professor Gizmo had a excellent concept. He dipped a paintbrush right into a combination of suitable for eating hues extracted from the planet of cookies and painted the rocket with a colourful pattern of swirls.

Professor emerge as very eager to percentage his invention and decrease decrease lower back to Earth. He met a quirky gardener Daisy. Daisy changed into specialised in growing notable plant life, and Professor Gizmo knew the right way to combine their competencies.

Chapter 15: Wallet

Professor Gizmo designed a greenhouse and requested Daisy's assist to boom cookie plants. Together, they planted cactus-formed cookies which sprouted into complete sized cactus vegetation with cookie thorns.

To preserve their ft comfortable in the direction of their gardening activity, they wore socks made from magical, self-adjusting material. These socks routinely tailor-made to any environment, providing endless comfort and hilarious foot dances.

Word in their unique gardening spread a protracted manner and big, attracting curious fanatics and adventurers. Visitors started out out journeying their greenhouse, having binoculars to look at the amazing cookie vegetation.

Professor Gizmo additionally displayed innovative pockets which become capable of storing and categorizing seeds primarily based totally on their sorts and flavors.

As people had been giggling, Professor Gizmo and Daisy couldn't face up to joining them. They grabbed a colorful skipping rope and commenced skipping in rhythm on the equal time as planting new cookie seeds.

Professor Gizmo and Daisy took breaks from gardening to enjoy a non violent fishing session with canon fashioned fishing rod designed thru Professor Gizmo.

They measured their cookie flowers' growth the usage of a tape degree enchanted with musical charms. With every length, the tape degree emitted melodic chimes making their gardening intervals enjoy like musical concert events.

Professor Gizmo and Daisy used flower vases to show their cookie flora. The vases now not first-class displayed the beauty of the cookie however additionally emitted a faint aroma enticing website visitors to take a more in-depth look.

When they wanted a wreck they finished with Rubik's Cube made from chocolate squares. They furthermore saved licking the Rubik's Cube to experience the chocolate.

Professor Gizmo and Daisy determined to journey their skateboard thru the cookie lawn in which they observed a hidden treasure chest buried underneath the soil. There was a set of T-shirts with a unique cookie-themed format within the treasure subject.

As their gardening adventures persisted, Professor Gizmo utilized his calculator to degree the cookie flora' growth expenses and calculate the quality watering and daytime ranges. The calculator modified into made on floor and modified into so massive that they had to jump on the buttons to perform the calculations.

They harvested harvesting their cookie vegetation with magical kitchen knife. The knife emitted a mild glow each time it came into touch with a ripe cookie plant, supporting them to become aware of the sweetest cookies.

Professor Gizmo and Daisy used dumbbells to sharpen their knife on every occasion required.

The Professor Gizmo designed an alarm which emitted dinosaur roaring sound each time a person tried to enter their cookie garden with out their permission. Whenever a person entered their cookie lawn, a dinosaur sitting on a big duration globe ought to come out of a cave and roar very loudly. Their alarm modified into very scary however saved their garden.

Chapter 16: Soccer Ball

You like watching stars and you've got ordinary a canon sized Telescope close to your mattress room window. On a Sunday, when you have been looking celebrity thru the telescope you decided a coffee maker shaped moon orbiting the earth. You have been amazed as properly you have been very glad which you have decided a new moon of Earth.

You without delay ran up on your girlfriends Maya's house to inform her approximately your new discovery. When you reached her home you located that she modified into mendacity on a Hammock and swinging.

The Hammock turned into tied amongst big sized paint brushes that have been constant with the brushing recommendations upwards. The brushes were swaying within the air due to wind and swinging the Hammock.

There had been many stunning flora throughout the hammock that have been making the scene very romantic. The vegetation vegetation were falling from the sky and had been amassing round hammock.

You started out gathering the flower plant life and started arranging them in flowerpots all over the paint brushes and hammock to make it appearance extra lovely. As you had been arranging vegetation, you noticed a fixed of large honeybees coming. To your astonishment, all of the honey bees had been sporting huge sized Sunglasses.

You proper now took out your Laptop and began out trying to find massive honeybees on Google because you in no manner noticed such big honeybees. Google cautioned carrying a entire frame fit for protection from honeybees. Just while you have been considering a manner to get full frame suit, you remembered that you had been having few such fits at your house.

You right away blew whistle and a horse got here taking walks to you who converted in to bicycle and you proper now jumped on the bicycle and commenced paddling it. You reached domestic and brought suits for yourself and your woman pal.

When you wore suits, you seemed like strolling guitars and started out out playing with each particular filling the air with gentle tune. All the honeybees started out dancing to your tunes. You have been amazed to appearance that all the honeybees had been dancing in synchronism.

As your track crammed the air, it began raining. All the honeybees stopped dancing and accumulated below a huge sized seashore umbrella in the lawn location to shield them from the rain. But they regardless of the truth that saved twirling and dancing. You and your woman buddy loved their impromptu live performance and burst into laughter.

To seize their superb overall performance you took out a mag out of your laptop bag and began writing about the honeybee's specific live performance. You stuffed many pages and you knew that many human beings will look at the story with disbelief.

Feeling satisfied with the wonders that they'd witnessed, the you every decided to put together dinner a few food as you began feeling hungry. You each donned chef's hats, started whipping the cream thru using a hard and speedy of dumbbells as unconventional stirrers.

After having food and some rest, you and your female friend determined to head on an journey trip into the woods. You held compass on your hand and have been exploring the dense wooded area. Your female pal became having a bull commonplace backpack on her again. You all at once stumbled upon a treasure field and determined historic foldable Binoculars.

You had by no means visible such binoculars and apparently you picked up the binoculars, wiped easy them and attempted to use it. You have been surprised to look that the binoculars have been in top situation and you can see an extended manner gadgets very clearly. Your girl buddy folded the binoculars and saved in her backpack.

Time surpassed with the aid of the usage of very fast however you have been absolutely misplaced in playing the instant. Suddenly the alarm clock commenced as quickly the clock touched 6.00PM. The sound of the alarm clock turn out to be like a roaring dinosaur. You began returning to domestic right away.

On returning, you have been feeling thirsty and as the monkey understood your feelings, it gave you water bottles with sparkling water in it. When you drank water from the bottle, you felt smooth and recharged another time. Your lady pal moreover felt the same and you every shared one bottle each.

After returning, you both favored to preserve your precious recollections, so that you created a mystical picture body. It modified into like a time gadget. Whenever you inserted a photo inside the magical body, the body transported you again in time so you may want to relive the antique moments.

To add a totally final contact of playfulness on your exceptional day, you took achieved football at the side of your lady friend. It changed into a mystical soccer ball. You decided that by way of kicking the football ball, you may deliver secret love messages to every different. Your football fits changed into amusing conversations, developing a game inside a sport and improving intimacy among you and your girl buddy.

Exercise-five

Hot air balloon

Roller skates

Camping tent

Surfboard

Telescope

Motorcycle

Aliens

Sailboat

Subway map

Compass

Trampoline

Zip line

Peacock

Train charge rate tag

Roller coaster

Hammock

Jet ski

Piranha

Spaceship

Water gun

You have an adventurous nature with wild imaginations. One sunny day, you stumbled upon a difficult and speedy of awesome gadgets that may take you to the most hilarious and surprising adventures.

You located a heat air balloon hidden away on your storeroom shed. You are not aware of its magical electricity to supply needs. You needed that you can fly in the warm air balloon and all of a unexpected you decided yourself flying over a sea entire of hungry sharks.

After crossing the present day air balloon descended in a deserted area and it became pain all spherical but no longer a few factor else. You wanted you can have roller skates so you may want to skip the abandoned area very rapid. Immediately your feet have been adorned with magical curler skates which propelled you ahead with exhilarating pace.

You reached the beach proper away and decided a adorable location to pitch a tenting tent from you backpack on the seashore. Suddenly you determined a large crocodile crawled slowly to you and said - " Hi, might you want to revel in the waves?". You have grow to be horrified that the crocodile will consume you but in your marvel, it transformed to a big Surfboard.

You cherished surfing for about an hour and again to the seaside. While sunbathing, you took out your magical Telescope which could see the far off items very honestly. As you focused your telescope on the ocean, you may see some massive octopus have been the use of bikes. It end up a peculiar motor cycle with massive drums geared up on every sides and its wheel were geared up with strips to thrust the water

As the Sun descend, the excessive tide began out and your tent become submerged so you taken secure haven on a Tree house near the timber alongside the seaside. While mendacity in the tree house, you seemed via a telescope and began exploring the distance and found a hidden galaxy complete of dancing extraterrestrial beings.

Eager to enroll in their extraterrestrial celebration, you hopped on a motorcycle which had wings and grow to be capable of fly. When you throttled it, the motorbike lifted off the floor propelling you thru location and time, in that you danced with the extraterrestrial beings.

Your adventures persisted and also you stumbled upon a sailboat that could navigate now not outstanding the ocean but moreover the subway. With a subway map in hand, you sailed thru the underground tunnels with the sailboat floating gracefully at the tracks.

Using a compass that pointed to the silliest places, you arrived at a trampoline park wherein gravity defied physics. You started performing gravity-defying flips and tips which brought approximately the opportunity site visitors to chortle at you.

While leaping, you all at once determined a zip line stretched at some point of the town, connecting skyscrapers and landmarks. You soared through the air, whooping and hollering as you zipped beyond startled flying peacocks and onlookers.

One of the peacock surpassed over you a paranormal educate rate charge tag granting you get right of entry to to a curler coaster train. As you rode the teach, the track twisted and grew to end up, looping spherical trees and via tunnels, reworking right right into a hilarious curler coaster journey.

You unexpectedly jumped from the roller coaster and landed right into a large hammock suspended between two palm trees on a sandy seaside. You attempted to take some rest however you had no idea that the hammock had the energy to transform right into a jet ski with a unmarried command. You zoomed throughout the waves, your laughter blending with the splashing water and sparkling delight you by no means had earlier than.

Suddenly you observed a big piranha following you and were horrified. The piranha had big tooth and saved its mouth huge open to bite you. You sped the ski jet with whole throttle.

Suddenly a large ramp emerged from the water and also you ran the ski jet at the ramp and landed in a large spaceship full of astronauts who've been searching you from the distance and giggling at you.

They held large water weapons complete of colored water and that they started out shooting at you with colored water jets as fast as you landed in the spaceship. You had been truly soaking wet in coloured water and couldn't recognize yourself even as you noticed within the replicate. You moreover joined the astronauts in laughing. Suddenly you've got been thrown from the spaceship and fell down in the world. When you opened your eyes, you placed yourself fallen from the mattress. You understood that it modified into all a dream, a memorable dream entire of surprises, fun and excitement.

Exercise-6

Toaster

Chess set

Hammock

Paint roller

Ceramic mug

Sombrero hat

Tablet charger

Bicycle bell

Harmonica

Camping tent

Compass

Travel suitcase

Yoga ball

Money jar

Beach umbrella

Binoculars

Wall clock

Stainless metal thermos

Magnetic fridge clips

Basketball

This listing has been given so you can exercise and take a look at your modern visualization. Create a very unique tale the usage of the above phrases and take a look at your success.

www.ingramcontent.com/pod-product-compliance
Lightning Source LLC
Chambersburg PA
CBHW071448080526
44587CB00014B/2032